If It's Raining

This Must Be the Weekend

If *It's Raining*

This Must Be
the Weekend

NANCY STAHL

ANDREWS AND McMEEL, INC.
A Universal Press Syndicate Company
KANSAS CITY

Library of Congress Cataloging in Publication Data
Stahl, Nancy, 1937-
   If it's raining this must be the weekend.
   1. Women—Anecdotes, facetiae, satire, etc.
2. Family—Anecdotes, facetiae, satire, etc.
I. Title.
PN6231.W6S68   818:.5:407   78-27009
ISBN 0-8362-1114-6

January 2

Most people break New Year's resolutions by January 17, simply because they have greatly overestimated their capabilities.

Let's face it, anyone unable to do fifteen push-ups, lose twenty-five pounds, or make a lasting contribution to world peace last year has precious little hope of being able to accomplish it this year, either.

No, New Year's resolutions must be confined to smaller, more easily controlled foibles, sprinkled liberally with reminders not to repeat actions which were so asinine at the time that there is no possibility of their happening again anyway.

For instance, this year I resolve to:

1. Practice preventive dentistry at two o'clock in the afternoon, rather than phoning Dr. Epstein in the middle of his son's Bar Mitzvah.

2. Tell the children the facts of life, at least those I remember.

3. Turn the mattress every three months.

4. Wash all the silverware after meals, even the spoons which nobody used.

5. Take down the outside Christmas lights before Easter.

By the same token, I resolve not to:

1. Appear in the supermarket in white anklets and hair rollers, no matter how badly we need curry powder.

2. Put coffee grounds down the sink.

3. Tell any jokes unless I am sure I remember the punch line.

4. Stay up till 2:30 A.M. to watch *Godzilla vs. The Thing.*

5. Stick a fork in the toaster.

6. Take any miracle drug unless given proof that all of its original users passed away quietly in their sleep at the age of seventy-three.

7. Ride in an elevator whose safety inspection sticker has expired.

8. Lick the blades of an electric mixer that is still plugged in.

☂ January 4

I truly admire people who love to entertain, people who are eager to share the warmth and hospitality of their homes. People who know instinctively who to invite.

By the time we have compiled a semiappropriate guest list, I find myself regarding the whole idea of entertaining with the air of heady expectation I usually reserve for a dental appointment.

It is considered important to ensure that there will be a similarity of background among your guests. While providing a common bond is perhaps a safe course of action, there exists the dreadful possibility that our guests will spend the entire evening discussing their kidney dialysis.

The obvious alternative is to aim for a delicious mixture of introverts and extroverts, intellectuals and bohemians. While such rich catholicity of taste and philosophy may indeed elicit fascinating repartee, it may instead be rather disconcerting when our guests discover that they share absolutely no similar tastes or interests. In fact, after three painful hours, they may

If It's Raining

realize that the single thing which they have in common is a friendship with us, a fact which they each silently resolve to rectify the very next day.

I know that we should invite the twelve couples we have owed invitations since last July and, in one grand gesture, wipe our entire social slate clean. Unfortunately, the only reason that we haven't as yet returned these invitations is that we vividly remember what a dismal time we had at *their* parties. Which leaves me with the depressing prospect of stuffing mushroom caps for twenty-four people I can't stand.

Instead, should we perhaps invite twenty-four new people who would, in turn, feel obligated to issue a return invitation? Witty, charming people who will hopefully wipe *their* social slates clean with a poolside extravaganza next July.

After deciding who to invite, the next problem is what to do with the guests. My problem is that I do not like party games.

In fact, I resent investing three hours at the hairdresser and five dollars on a new pair of support stockings only to spend the entire evening scampering around with a thumbtack taped to my forehead, breaking balloons.

It is even more traumatic to have a navel orange thrust under my chins, especially since the game invariably requires me to pass it to a man who is six-foot-eight and has no more chin than a turtle.

January 6

The only graceful way to camouflage the embarrassing stigma of dining alone in a restaurant is to bring along a paperback, thus implying to my fellow patrons that I have sought my solitary state by choice, preferring to peruse a classic piece of literature than to indulge in insipid social discourse.

A friend of mine from Newark claims that she has solved the solitary-dining problem neatly by assuming the role of a princess recently exiled from a little-known Eastern European principality.

Wearing fifteen dollars worth of cheap rhinestone jewelry, a slinky black dress, and a mantilla, she sweeps in carrying a copy of an Estonian newspaper that she found in the ladies room of a Boston coffee house in 1956. When the waiter comes to take her order, she smiles wanly, points to filet mignon, and murmurs "Biftik—rare."

Between bites, she scans the newspaper, sighs tragically, and crosses herself repeatedly with her dessert fork.

Not only does she have a marvelous time, but her waiter invariably refuses to accept a tip.

 *January 8*

I have never felt the same about plants since I read that they have nervous systems which enable them to experience anxiety, joy, and—quite possibly—lust.

I've always *liked* plants, mind you. But heretofore I've regarded them rather like potholders—useful and decorative, but hardly something I could train to fetch the paper or catch mice.

In view of the vast body of knowledge which has recently emerged, it is no longer possible to regard plants as simply decorating necessities. Giving them bonemeal and tap water is not enough. If they are to thrive, plants need soothing music, inspirational verse, and verbal encouragement. Like petulant children, they must be cajoled into blooming. "Believe me, Harry, you'll feel better once you bud."

Since plants have come into their own, emotionally-speaking, anyone owning a philodendron can never feel himself to

4   *If It's Raining*

be completely alone again.

While this situation may be all very well should the owner be skittish about burglars, it presents a distressing prospect to those individuals who view being completely alone as an erotic pleasure second only to having their kneecaps stroked with goose feathers.

Personally, I find it next to impossible to cavort about the house wearing nothing but a pair of red woolen ski socks and risk offending the sensibilities of an African Violet.

☂ January 9

I'm actually all in favor of couples living together before they get married.

But only if you have to share your illicit prenuptial bliss with a semi-housetrained puppy, two children with the flu, and a water heater that goes kerchook, kerchonk, kerchonk all night.

Under those conditions you could *really* get to know each other.

That's what "compatible" is all about. After all, you know from your first date that it feels good when he rubs your neck. What really counts is how he reacts when the baby throws up on his Harris tweed sport coat. While marriage is made up of a good deal of neck rubbing, there's also a substantial amount of throwing up involved, and if he's going to stomp his feet and throw things when it happens, well, it's just as well to know about it beforehand.

And if the fact that you wear a chin strap and cut your toe-nails in bed is going to bother him, now is the time for it all to come out in the open.

It might be a good idea to arrange for a power failure, too. Eating by candlelight is one thing. Shaving by candlelight is quite another matter. Especially when you have shaved your legs with the razor first.

If you can manage it, it might be handy to have a drippy faucet for him to cope with. Lacking that, flush a diaper down the toilet. See whether he goes all pale and trembly when you hand him a wrench and a plunger.

Engage in funfilled activities like rearranging the living room furniture, putting up storm windows, and wallpapering the bathroom ceiling.

If you find that you can still stand the sight of each other after two weeks of this, then you probably have at least a fighting chance of muddling through till your golden wedding anniversary.

☂ January 11

My friend Marjorie has had a difficult time adjusting to the implications of the Women's Liberation Movement.

"I'm just a *housewife!*" she would wail. "I could have been a *surgeon!*" It did little good to point out that few, if any, surgeons insist on picking up calves liver with tongs because it feels "ishy."

Marjorie eventually took to refusing to accept her role. She baked pies only at night, put them in hat boxes, and insisted that she bought them at the A&P.

Suddenly, however, an abrupt transformation occurred.

"I took a course called 'The Managerial Perspective as Applied to Housework.' It changed my life. I never realized the fact that I am chief policy formulator, head decision-maker, an expert in domestic analysis."

"You bake super pies, too," I observed.

"I'm talking about roles," Marjorie explained. "My ability to appraised logistical dilemmas."

If It's Raining

"Like folding a contour sheet!" I exclaimed.

"More than that. Do you realize the importance of analytic appraisal?"

"Like whether to soak a mustard stain in hot water or cold water?" I asked.

"In the area of food preparation alone," she continued, "the aspects of financial management are critical. One must achieve creative artistry, which is a true challenge."

"Especially when it comes to canned peas," I agreed. "Tell me, did they happen to teach you how to overcome negative attitudes toward leftover tuna casserole?"

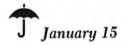 *January 15*

When women's magazines aren't exhorting me to knit my own lamp shades or create memorable holiday centerpieces out of the cardboard cylinders from toilet paper rolls, they invariably resort to testing my marriage: Does he bring you gin and tonic in the bathtub? Do you tuck lovenotes into his lunch bucket?

In the interest of realism, I have devised the following marriage test:

To be answered by women:

1. Your husband bought you a black lace negligee, size seven. Would you exchange it for: (a) a blue flannel Mother Hubbard nightie, size sixteen, or (b) a new toaster?

2. Three separate fortunetellers have predicted that you will be married twice. Do you: (a) cancel your order for monogrammed sheets, or (b) begin introducing him as "my first husband"?

3. There is a very young, blonde voice on the telephone wanting to speak to your husband. Would you say: (a) "Could

you call back? He's busy bathing our six adorable children," or (b) "You'll have to wait a minute. He's busy cutting his corns"?

To be answered by men:
1. Your wife asks "Am I as attractive as when we first met?" Do you answer (a) "Yeah, I guess so," or (b) "More so. All those lines give your face character"?
2. Your wife complains that there is a big, hungry spider on the ceiling. Would you (a) hand her a rolled-up newspaper, or (b) hand her a fly?
3. Your wife loans you her section of the newspaper, saying "You have to read this article by George Plopnik on topless restaurants." Do you: (a) Read the article, then return it, saying "What's so funny about that?" or (b) skim the Plopnik article, then become engrossed in a feature on the rehabilitation of juvenile delinquents, leaving her nothing to read but a sixteen-page flyer on sale-priced snow tires?

In each case, (a) is the correct choice and is worth five points. Give yourself one point for choosing (b). Combine your scores.

18-30—You will probably be together another thirty years. Isn't that peachy?

6-14—You need an outside interest. Have you tried creating memorable holiday centerpieces out of the cardboard cylinders from toilet paper rolls?

January 16

I recently read a magazine article entitled "Play 'Consequences' With Your Child." The author went on to explain that "Consequences" involves asking your child "What would happen if . . . ," thus urging him to develop his reasoning powers.

If It's Raining

Playing "Consequences" with our children is a bit like giving Michelangelo a paint-by-number set. They have dedicated their entire preadolescent lives to determining vital issues such as: What would happen if I dropped jelly beans down the hot air register? If I put caramels in the toaster? If I flushed my rubber duck down the toilet? If I cut off my eyelashes?

Of course, the whole trick to playing the game of "Consequences" lies in keeping everything at a purely theoretical level.

"What would happen if Mommy didn't use a potholder to take the biscuits out of the oven?" I asked.

"You'd burn your hand."

"That's right!" I beamed. "Then what would happen?"

"You'd say %$*!"

"How many times have I told you not to say that word?"

"I didn't say it. I said that you'd say it."

Determining to avoid personal issues, I tried the game again the next day. "What would happen if the electricity went off?"

"We wouldn't be able to watch TV or shave or wash dishes or open cans. And my worms would melt."

"What worms?"

"The worms I put in the freezer last summer. I wanted to see what would happen if . . . "

🌂 *January 17*

One of the joys of family life lies in coming together at the end of the day and exchanging experiences with those you love.

In our house, the exchange takes the form of a game of verbal one-upmanship known as "Your Day Was a Picnic

Compared With Mine."

"You should have *seen* the traffic on Eisenhower Boulevard!" I began last night. "It took me an hour and fifteen minutes to get home!"

"You think that's bad," retorted my daughter. "My bike got a flat and I had to walk two miles home from school."

"That's nothing," replied her brother. "Some gangster hijacked our school bus and got it up to 137 miles an hour on the freeway. If he hadn't sideswiped a dairy truck, we'd all be in Albuquerque by now."

"I tried a new place for lunch," I announced. "The food was rotten, and the prices were exorbitant."

"You think that's bad," my daughter said. "In our cafeteria some girl found a cockroach in her chocolate milk."

"That's nothing," insisted my son. "Our cafeteria has been closed down by the Board of Health. The entire fifth grade died from eating catfood sandwiches."

"You know, it's no fun being a working woman," I sighed. "Nobody appreciates you."

"Being in junior high is worse," insisted my daughter. "Nobody understands you."

"That's nothing!" bellowed my son. "Nobody believes a word I say!"

☂ *January 18*

"You'll go into the hospital on Monday and be out by late Tuesday morning," the doctor explained. "There's really nothing to it," he added, patting my hand.

"*You* say there's nothing to it," I snapped. "It's not *your* ovaries they're tinkering with!"

Like any sensible person, I have studiously avoided any prolonged contact with hospitals.

If It's Raining

For one thing, I hate the way they smell. It isn't *just* the smell, mind you. Beauty shops don't smell all that great either, but no one ever died from getting a permanent wave.

When I arrived at the hospital, I was amazed to discover that the entire main floor was done in burgundy and olive carpeting with modern pictures, indirect lighting, and huge potted palms, giving the entire room the air of the lobby of a two-star resort hotel.

"I'd like a room," I whispered to the girl at the desk.

"Do you have a reservation?" she inquired.

"Stahl," I murmured. "Ovaries."

It was at this point that the resemblance to a resort hotel ended abruptly. They whisked me to a lab, banded my arm as they would a migratory bird, and forcibly induced me to part with several specimens of bodily fluids.

It wasn't only my room, a singularly sterile cubicle overlooking the hospital parking lot, that destroyed the illusion; I know of few hotels which demand that you sign a paper releasing them from any obligation whatsoever should you, during the next twenty-four hours, either have your car stolen or die.

An hour before the operation, the surgeon inquired: "How are you feeling?"

"More important, how are *you* feeling?" I asked nervously. "I mean, you *did* get a good night's sleep, didn't you? You look pretty fit," I observed, "except for that hicky on your neck."

"That's nothing," he assured me. "I just nicked myself shaving," he snickered, nudging me jovially in the ribs.

Admittedly, my recollection of this dialogue is rather garbled, as all morning a veritable parade of people had been poking needles into all exposed parts of my anatomy. By the time I arrived at the operating room, I was grinning idiotically and insisting that I was the Duchess of Windsor.

One hour after the operation, I had ceased grinning.

"How do you feel?" my roommate inquired solicitously.

"Sick," I replied. "How else?"

"Would you like a beer?" she asked. "I have a six-pack

hidden in my bedpan. It makes a swell ice bucket. Help your-self to some pretzels. They're behind the TV set."

"I want to go home!" I wailed.

"Whatever for? It's raining ice balls out there. Personally, I *love* the hospital. The meals are no worse than your own and you get your back rubbed twice a day."

☂ *January 20*

There are some intimate subjects which one simply does not discuss.

Oh, I don't mean sex. Even my mother talks about sex.

In fact, she taught me all about sex. What she didn't teach me was how to shave my legs. Nobody teaches a thirteen-year-old girl how to shave. They just hand her a razor.

For the past twenty-five years, I've searched women's magazines for instructions, but all I even find is self-help arti-cles entitled "Make the Most of Your Nose" and meat loaf recipes.

I've tried hanging around bathrooms watching men shave. While the basic principle is the same, men don't have shin bones on their faces or, for that matter, any area of face where one ill-considered swipe of the razor will peel off a strip of skin one-eighth-inch wide and fourteen inches long.

I have yet to resolve the basic dilemma of where women should shave. Shaving during one's bath seems like a logical first choice, but it rather defeats the purpose of meticulous per-sonal hygiene to emerge from the tub covered from the neck down with tiny brown hairs and globs of Rapid Shave.

While men shave in the bathroom sink, I know of very few mature women who are physically capable of putting one foot up in a washbowl. I know even fewer who, once in, could get out again. Not only is there a vast degree of physical trauma involved in having one foot stuck in a washbowl for six hours, but there is even greater emotional trauma in having her loved one chortle "Henry, you'll have to excuse the funny way old Mildred is walking, but you'll never guess . . . "

☂ January 26

In our house, the garbage bag goes out when it is full.

Unfortunately, "full" is an arbitrary word, applying generally to a plastic bag so crammed with moldy bread heels, Kentucky Fried Chicken bones, and pizza crusts that it not only smells like a dirty turtle bowl, but there's no slack on which to place a twist-tie.

The bag is left in this unenviable state until the next person attempts to empty a handful of peanut shells into it, whereupon three grapefruit rinds full of cigarette butts immediately dislodge and skitter across the kitchen floor.

While it is fairly simple to pick the extra garbage off the floor and reapportion it into a second bag, leaving the original bag empty enough to accept a twist-tie, once you attempt to lift it you discover a severed soup can lid has sliced a three-inch gash in the bottom, and six cups of wet coffee grounds are dribbling onto your shoe.

Clasping your hand quickly over the bottom of the bag temporarily relieves the leakage problem, but the only permanent solution lies in depositing the bag into another bag, preferably before the soup can lid succeeds in severing your right index finger.

☂ January 27

In these days of skyrocketing food costs, I have found that is is essential to make a list of the items I intend to buy.

A list not only prevents me from intemperate buying, but it adds an aura of efficiency, and, with luck, will draw my fellow-shoppers' attention away from the fact that I have forgotten to change out of my bedroom slippers.

A list has certain drawbacks, however.

1. You must remember to bring it. It does precious little good to spend the entire morning noting down the ingredients for "Rainy Day Shepherd's Pie" and rummaging through the cupboard shaking bottles of bleach to determine whether you have enough for another week, only to arrive at the grocery store and discover that you've left the list on top of the refrigerator.

2. The list must be decipherable. While many women employ an elaborate code to protect the list from being translated, should it be confiscated, it is most distressing to realize that you have absolutely no idea what "PRTD. MST.!" might be.

Making a list is only part of the battle, however.

It is equally vital to visit the grocery store only when you have just completed a twelve-course meal and are so completely weighted down with starch that you can barely waddle.

It is easy to spot someone who has made the mistake of arriving at the store hungry and "listless." She is the woman who is guiltily unloading a cart containing a half-gallon of fudge ripple ice cream, three dozen Snickers bars, and a half-eaten box of Hostess Cupcakes.

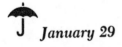

January 29

I enjoy having overnight guests.

Not only does the prospect of entertaining company provide the necessary impetus for long neglected household chores such as cleaning the gnats out of the overhead light fixture, but the contents of the refrigerator experience a notable improvement in quality when overnight guests arrive.

But the fact remains that, unlike dinner guests who are entertained by candlelight and carefully confined to the living room, dining room, and powder room, overnight guests have the run of the house. And although they may not remark on it, they will definitely notice a furry green ring in the bathtub.

It would never do to let a guest suspect how you really live, so when the next one announces an imminent visit, I must remember to do the following:

1. Check the medicine cabinet for potentially embarrassing medicines and items of personal hygiene.

2. Clean all the cigarette butts out of the rubber plant.

3. Buy new toothbrushes.

4. Remove *The Joy of Sex* from the night stand. Substitute *Wuthering Heights*.

5. Iron a set of sheets.

6. Check the grooves of the window in the guest room for dead flies.

7. Invest in two-ply bathroom tissue.

But I also must remember that while such elaborate preparations are designed to make a guest feel at home, it will never do to create such a degree of comfort that he loses all desire to return home. After five days, it is perfectly proper to temper hospitality with the insistence that guests take out the garbage, feed the dog, and clean the furry green ring out of the bathtub.

 *January 30*

The challenge of creating a memorable gastronomic experience out of two cups of leftover roast pork does not exactly set my libido a-twitter. Generally speaking, I would rather run around the block stark naked when it's fifteen degrees below zero than cook dinner. Of course, it's all academic anyway, as I've never been offered the choice.

Lately, however, our daughter has begun to regard the oven as something more than a place to dry her tennis shoes. I supervised her early efforts and offered helpful suggestions. It soon became apparent that I lacked a certain objectivity and was prone to gasping and wringing my hands when she sliced a tomato.

Now I just sit in the living room with a tourniquet and a fire extinguisher, resolving not to take a bite of anything until I've counted her fingers.

I must admit that she's very innovative. Cookbooks inhibit her; she creates as she goes along. Meatball and banana casserole with chocolate biscuits was one impromptu offering. And none of us will ever forget the pork chops with blueberry-clam sauce. She had wanted to flame them with twelve-year-old cognac, but she had used it all making the mashed potatoes.

"What's for supper?" my husband asked.

"I'm not sure. It smells like sauteed rubber bands."

"It couldn't be. She served that just last night."

While her Daddy and I wouldn't dream of complaining, our son is apt to call a spade a spade and announce that he'd rather eat nightcrawlers than pork chops with blueberry-clam sauce.

"Mom and Dad like it. Don't you?" she asked us. We nodded solemnly, palming our pork chops under the table and attempting to interest the dog in them. He shuddered and left the room.

"Mom and Dad love you. They have to say it's good. I don't even like you very much, so I don't have to be polite."

February 2

I just read an article which began with the startling statement, "Your furniture says a lot about you."

I have spent ten grueling years attempting to convince the children not to reveal our private physical peculiarities, petty disputes, or bank overdrafts. Now I find that I should have concentrated on the blabbermouths in the living room. In fact, all that our assorted furnishings have in common is the ability to badmouth us:

Danish modern end tables, circa 1965, badly scarred: Teeth marks on legs of these early artifacts indicate regrettable lack of parental discipline. White ring on square table, evidently vestige of long-ago holiday merrymaking, shows traces of being treated with every chemical known to science. Ring regularly reappears like the Ghost of Christmas Past. Spot of wax on step table indicates that owners do not own a candle snuffer. Since everyone receives at least six sterling silver candle snuffers as wedding gifts, they undoubtedly never bothered to get married at all.

Early American wing chair, circa 1970, grape Popsicle stain on underside of cushion: Slightly later period, the fact that said chair has springs indicates increasing affluence, but tendency to pander to offspring still apparent if you turn cushion over.

French Provincial stereo, circa 1973, seven cigarette burns on top, spray can of furniture polish and filthy dust cloth inside: Cigarette burns indicate that one conscience-ridden spouse attempted to evade responsibility for the other contracting emphysema by the ill-considered ploy of hiding all the ashtrays. Furniture polish can an impressive housekeeping gesture, but has been empty for three months.

Italian love seats, circa 1976, covered in immaculate gold velvet: Relatively new, therefore use restricted to those bearing notarized affidavit attesting to personal hygiene. No one has bothered to acquire sufficient documentation, as the love seats aren't particularly comfortable, anyway.

☂ *February 5*

I am sure that the main reason so many first-born children become famous is the onus of having to live up to those early reviews in their own baby books.

The life and times of our first-born child are chronicled in an elaborate pink satin volume with twelve smirking cherubs and a spot of what looks like strained peas on the cover. Every word that she ever managed to lisp out is documented like the Congressional Record, while truly momentous occasions, like the compelling saga of her first sneeze, run to three pages.

Slightly heavier than *Webster's New International Dictionary,* her baby book bulges with envelopes full of teeth, wisps of hair, and fingernail parings. Our daughter is probably the only girl in town who could take her own umbilical cord to school for Show-and-Tell.

I suppose that I saved these souvenirs because she was constantly doing *wonderful, exciting things* which I was terrified of forgetting. All mothers are alike in that respect. I know that my own mother would sooner part with her nose than relinquish a certain glutinous mass which she insists was

If It's Raining

once my rubber ducky.

This tendency to collect infantile memorabilia gradually wore off by the time our daughter was three or four years old and began doing *things* that were not *wonderful* or *exciting*, like dropping 150 miniature marshmallows down the heating duct and swallowing my best earrings, which I truly hoped to be able to forget just as soon as was possible. Besides, no one can bronze a pair of shoes after they have been flushed down the toilet.

February 6

Regarding child discipline, I favor the "early warning system," otherwise known as the "1-2-3 and you're out" approach.

Since I consider that first offenders are motivated by curiosity rather than malice, I deliver patient lectures with catchy titles such as "Why One Does Not Keep Dead Sparrows in Vegetable Crispers" and "Nice People Do Not Drink Their Bathwater."

Second offenders must be dealt with in a stern fashion, as they are generally testing your authority with a little game called "Let's See Whether She Really Means It," as in the following situation:

Child in muddy cowboy boots stands upright on the back of the sofa, grasps his nose between his thumb and forefinger, shrieks "Geronimo," and jumps into the seat cushion. The sofa bleats like a mortally wounded elk.

"Look, I've told you not to jump off the back of the sofa!"

"No you didn't. You just said not to jump off the back of the *chair!*"

"Well, I'm telling you now. If you do it one more time I'll send you right to bed." Notice that the child is thus being given freedom of choice. Of course, if it happens to be an hour past his bedtime already, he may realize that he not only has nothing to lose if he opts for a final jump, but in the ensuing crisis may very well avoid having to brush his teeth.

When confronting a child with a nasty alternative to continued obnoxious behavior, it is imperative to keep a bit of perspective and remember exactly who it is you are punishing. While "If you stick one more marble up the baby's nose, I'll make you stay in the house all weekend" may possibly restrain him, on the other hand, it very well may not. One more marble will leave you no alternative but to have him underfoot for the next forty-eight hours, whiling away his time by jumping off the piano while protesting, "No you didn't. You just said not to jump off of the sofa or the chair."

☂ *February 7*

I enjoy receiving a bunch of cut flowers. Since they are technically *in extremis* when I receive them, no one expects roses to live. It is only a matter of postponing the inevitable. Even though I dutifully go through the motions of shaving their stems daily, and plying them with aspirin and Vitamin C, after a week I know that no one will fault me for throwing the whole sodden, brownish mass down the garbage disposal.

On the other hand, a potted African Violet is *alive*, a supposedly *lasting gift*. Even after it has become *my* African Violet, and as such could, in theory, be chopped up for salad greens, the giver retains a certain proprietary interest in "Our African Violet's" well-being and feels entitled to poke his finger into the potting soil and make snide remarks about my watering habits.

The situation is even more tense when people insist on giving me a cutting off the ancestral ivy. This is a semireligious

　　　　　　　　　　　　　　　　　If It's Raining

ceremony which leaves me feeling a bit like Moses receiving the Ten Commandments. "Grandmother Nelson dug the parent plant from the Happy View Cemetery in Lincoln, Nebraska, in July, 1901," they will say. "We only give cuttings to our very dearest friends."

Resisting the urge to genuflect, I gaze despairingly at the sprig of ivy, which has begun to wilt in my sweaty palm. After a while, under the watchful eye of Grandma Nelson's shade, I dutifully plant the ivy in the exact type of soil recommended for heirloom ivy.

But even though I use nothing on it but seventy-eight-degree distilled water and spend all afternoon hauling it from one shaft of sunlight to another, it reacts just like a rose. Whenever we sit down to eat breakfast, decaying ivy leaves begin plummeting into our porridge. After a week I throw the whole sodden, brownish mass down the garbage disposal.

I have to admit that none of my best friends are potted plants. Anything that demands such care and feeding should have the decency to lick your hand or apologize when it dies.

Now my son—there's a talented green thumb.

Some children long for Santa to bring them shiny red wagons, hockey gloves, and toboggans. Others wistfully yearn for an electric train, a woodburning set, or the latest Judith Blume books. My son wanted a Venus Fly Trap this year.

Whatever the psychological significance of this request, it is definitely nothing upon which I care to speculate.

A Venus Fly Trap is an insectivorous plant which catches its prey like a steel trap. The two halves of the leaf, about the size of nickels, are hinged in the middle. When an insect walks on its surface, the leaf snaps shut, the toothed edges mesh, and the plant squeezes its victim against the digestive glands on the leaf surface until the insect's body is decomposed by enzymes. Yo ho ho.

A Venus Fly Trap cannot be purchased in this active state, however. It is native to North Carolina (and that's what I like about the South), from where it is exported in a dormant state. Encased in a plastic bag, the Venus Fly Trap exhibits all the intrinsic charm of a spider that has been run over by a skateboard.

With a modicum of luck, it will remain in this enviable state and can be simply thrown away in six weeks or so. Unfortunately, my son's Venus Fly Trap (which he named Fang) germinated into quivering life and soon began opening its revolting maw for food.

Fang, we soon discovered, can distinguish between living and dead objects (such as Cheerios), and exhibits utter disdain for the latter. While in mid-July we are plagued with veritable hordes of flying insects, it is a rare phenomenon to find a horsefly in February. Fortunately, our basement has become the Capistrano of the crawling insect world.

While Fang lacks a certain aesthetic appeal, I must admit he is doing an exemplary job on the silverfish problem. Besides, he is the only one of Santa's gifts that isn't either too small, broken, or out of "D" cell batteries.

February 10

"Fred and I are having a party two weeks from Saturday," the voice on the telephone said. "We were hoping that you folks could come."

"That sounds fine. Hold on just a minute while I check the calendar." (Checking the calendar is a cunning ploy to convince people that we are constantly in demand. Actually I don't have to check. I already know that our only social obligation for the next six weeks is to take the dog to the vet for a rabies booster.) "We're free that night," I said, trying to sound mildly surprised at the fact. "We'd love to come."

Unfortunately, being in the mood for a party is like being pregnant. At any given moment I can tell whether I am or I'm not. Two weeks from Saturday, who knows?

Two weeks from Saturday, as I gingerly applied lipstick

If It's Raining

over the cold sore on my upper lip, I felt definitely unpartyish.

"The Monster from the Black Lagoon," my husband announced glumly.

"Haven't you ever seen a cold sore?" I snarled.

"I mean on the eleven o'clock TV movie. Can't we stay home?"

"I hate to cancel out so late," I mused, "after I've shaved my legs and all. But I do have a little headache that I'll bet I could worry into a throbbing migraine by 10:45."

"Make it 10:30 to allow for traffic," he cautioned as we left.

But by 10:30 it became apparent that one of us was having a smashing time. Since I was being treated to a cost analysis of secondary sewage treatment systems in Los Angeles, it obviously wasn't me. My husband, however, was in deep conversation with a redhead who was wearing one of those push-me-up bras and looking at him as if he'd just discovered the wheel.

"I don't suppose that I still have a headache?" I asked him, temporarily disengaging myself from Los Angeles's sewage problems.

"Not on my account," he said hastily. "Besides, you did shave your legs and all."

☂ *February 11*

Every year, I find the remaining bits and pieces of Christmas decidedly depressing.

February is a grim enough month anyway without impaling my foot on a pine needle still imbedded, pointy end up, in the carpet, whenever I walk barefoot in the living room.

Having been on the receiving end of seven Christmas fruitcakes, we have been reduced to eating fruitcake sandwiches, French-fried fruitcake, and creamed fruitcake on buttered fruitcake points. Not only do they show no inclination to get stale, but their strength is like the strength of ten because their hearts are pure brandy. I made the mistake of throwing two cups of fruitcake crumbs outside for the birds last week. Half an hour later, six sparrows were staggering along the telephone wire singing "When It's Springtime in the Rockies" in close harmony, while a cardinal was Indian wrestling with a Siamese cat. And winning.

Our son has developed a musical fixation on Christmas carols. Here it is mid-February and there is still a partridge in his pear tree.

Every day we receive sternly worded documents from the local department stores, requesting that we pay for our December magnanimity, all of which has either broken, shrunk, or is sitting immobilized for want of fresh batteries.

Our outside lights are still hanging glumly from the roof. Only ten weeks ago, a heady infusion of holiday spirit enabled my husband to leap smartly from my shoulders onto an icy rooftop, wrap his legs around the chimney, and clip red flashing lights onto the shingles to spell out *Peace on Earth*. Five weeks ago, natural attrition had reduced their message to *Peace o Ear*. Last week when they further abridged themselves to a rather ridiculous *Pea*, I finally turned them off.

"At least you could replace the red bulb in the porch light," I said to my husband.

"Why? It looks festive."

"A red light over the door was festive two months ago. In February there is only one excuse for that light, and our area isn't even zoned for apartments!"

Especially depressing is the five hundred-piece jigsaw puzzle I purchased for the family as a present. Rather than the standard "Venice at Sunset" or "Miss December" variety, this puzzle is a giant gum ball machine.

Two things became obvious as soon as we began the puzzle late in the afternoon of December 27. First, one gum ball looks depressingly like another. Second, two-thirds of the puzzle is solid black.

Unfortunately, before we could adopt the sensible approach of simply shoving all 500 pieces into the trash can, my son put three pieces together, thus morally committing us to assembling the remaining 497. For the past eight weeks, we have eaten in the kitchen, standing up at the counter, the dining room table being completely covered with gum balls.

Now a jigsaw puzzle may be approached from either of two directions. Some maintain the philosophy that one must sit and stare speculatively at the puzzle, looking for a particular piece with the appropriate configuration. The other approach, based on the theory that seven monkeys sitting at seven typewriters will eventually type all of the books in the Library of Congress, consists of trying every piece in every hole.

Unfortunately, these two approaches are often incompatible in practice.

My son, the sitter, objects violently to his sister's shotgun approach.

"Those pieces don't go together," he protested last night.

"They do now!" she replied, hammering two gum balls violently with her fist.

"Anything worth doing is worth doing *right*, you jerk!" he bellowed.

"Maybe," I replied, "but unless we try shaving little bits off some of these pieces, we'll end up eating Thanksgiving dinner standing up in the kitchen."

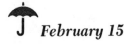 *February 15*

Every night at dinner, my children play a game entitled "Top News Story of the Day." It's a variation of the "If You Think Your Day Was Bad . . . " game, and the rules are simple. Whatever bit of folksy information my daughter reports, her younger brother must counterattack immediately by injecting a more bizarre incident, beginning with the words "That's nothing. Some kid in my class . . . "

This Must Be the Weekend

25

A typical exchange runs much along the following lines:

Laurie: "A guy in my class named Michael Harris got cross-country skis for Christmas."

Eric: "That's nothing. Some kid in my class got a three-hundred-speed bike for Christmas. It goes seven-thousand miles an hour. His mother is a black belt in karate, and his father is a Russian spy."

Laurie (desperately): "Carlene Shultz can burp at will."

Eric: "That's nothing. Some kid in my class can pull his eyes right out of their sockets, get a whole grapefruit in his mouth, and make his nose bleed by pulling on his earlobes."

Laurie, understandably miffed at being continually upstaged, will occasionally exhibit a bit of skepticism as to the authenticity of these events. For example:

Laurie: "Ritchie McGrath ate a fly today."

Eric: "That's nothing. Some kid in my class swallows rats."

Laurie: "Don't be dumb. Rats are too big to swallow."

Eric: "I didn't say big rats, smarty. He swallows little rats. Babies."

Laurie: "Sara Jenkins brought her basset hound to school today."

Eric: "That's nothing. Some kid in my class brought in his pet gorilla. I petted him and he let me feel his muscles."

Laurie: "Oh, brother!"

Eric: "What do *you* know? You don't even go to my school!"

☂ *February 18*

Over the years I have learned that motherhood is much like an austere religious order, the joining of which obligates one to relinquish all claims to personal possessions.

Not only is my badminton racquet referred to as "*The*

badminton racquet" and as such regularly loaned to friends, left in hedges, and used to strain the water out of the pan full of Kraft dinner, but the children fight over which one of them gets to chew up my last sheet of personalized stationery to make spitballs.

Just last week I bought a pair of black leather gloves to go with my good black coat. As I was dressing for a luncheon date yesterday, I saw my daughter through the bedroom window wearing my black gloves to school. There was nothing to do but wear her brown knit gloves. Just then I spied my son walking down the street in her brown knit gloves. I was the only woman to arrive at the luncheon wearing green and yellow snowflake mittens with one thumb unravelled.

Occasionally, however, there are opportunities to get a little of my own back.

Last night the children appeared clutching a pair of blue jeans which each adamantly insisted was his.

"All right," I declared. "I'll cut them in half. Each of you gets one leg." I reasoned that the rightful owner would love his jeans enough to relinquish his claim to save them. (This worked admirably for King Solomon in a dispute involving ownership of a baby.)

Unfortunately, as both children agreed to the division, King Solomon was forced to reverse his decision. It's one thing to chop a baby in two, but no wise king cuts up a pair of perfectly good jeans. He wears them himself, even if he can't quite zip them up.

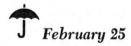 *February 25*

I am completely accustomed to feeling inferior.

I learned twenty years ago that not only was my prowess at simple stain removal woefully nonexistent, but that I lacked the ability to boil water without scorching it.

I have learned to live with my inadequacies.

But thanks to the candid approach recently adopted by even the most staid journalistic sentinels of womanhood, I find that I am equally ill-equipped emotionally.

It is frightening to envision the editorial upheavals that must have occurred at even the most hallowed publications. China-painting experts, origami geniuses, dried-flower impresarios—all must have been abruptly terminated in this new wave of women's journalism.

It is all very well to accept my inability to embroider my own pillow cases. I don't even *like* hand-embroidered pillow cases; the French knots always leave dents in my cheek. But it's quite another matter to discover that I am shamefully unassertive, psychologically repressed, and sexually naive.

It is most disconcerting to find that the very same people who tried—unsuccessfully, I might add—to instruct me in the intricacies of preventing the interfacing in my collar from curling, now are confiding that if I stop smoking, my sexual appetite will increase.

Don't get me wrong. An increased sexual appetite is without a doubt a Good Thing. But I can't help remembering what trouble I found myself in trying to interface my collar.

February 27

Somehow I had expected the Women's Liberation Movement to relieve me from the drudgery of housework.

But what Germaine Greer fails to point out is that just as the rain falls on both the just and unjust, so dust is no respecter of a raised consciousness.

As one must, of necessity, deal with housework, the following courses could raise apparent drudgery to a truly crea-

If It's Raining

tive level, commensurate with an emerging woman's newfound capabilities:

1. *The Managerial Perspective as Applied to the Linen Closet 101:* This course stresses appraisal of the existing situation, as well as covering policy formation regarding the use of shelf paper. Advanced students with a strong mathematical background will benefit from Course 102: *Solving the Logistical Dilemma of Folding a Contour Sheet.*

2. *Interfacing with Milkmen 310:* Interpersonal transaction is emphasized in this course. Stroke theory is offered as a medium for obtaining specials on cottage cheese two weeks after the offer has expired.

3. *Stain Appraisal 440:* The decision-making aspects involved in the use of hot or cold water are emphasized. Attention is given to the pragmatic approach to mustard and blood, as well as the Freudian implications of "Ring Around the Collar."

4. *Workshop in Leftover Cookery 560:* Truly invaluable for the aspiring financial manager, this results-oriented approach to peas, mashed potatoes, and bacon fat begins with a comprehensive overview of existing materials, examines restructuring techniques to achieve creative expression, and finally addresses itself to methods of overcoming negativity, rigidity, and natural aggressiveness to Shepherd's Pie.

Instead of advanced education, one can always opt for a maid.

While it isn't easy to get hired help, it is even more difficult to get rid of hired help.

If a maid proves herself to be lazy, surly, and unbearably slovenly, I simply assume that it was my own fault for having hired such an incompetent in the first place. Her presence becomes a cross that I must bear, rather like a weird relative who collects peach pits and, unless watched carefully, runs down the street stark naked, barking and chasing cars.

My first experiment with household help was named, as best as I could ever discover, Nijishruljhi. Whatever her linguistic abilities were, they stopped well short of English.

Ignoring the unmade beds and greasy oven, Nijishruljhi

spent her entire first day removing the mineral deposits from the holes of the shower head with a straight pin.

Using a series of expansive gestures, I tried to convey the fact that I desired a more macrocosmic approach to housecleaning.

The next Wednesday I arrived home to find that she had ripped out eighty square yards of wall-to-wall carpeting and was waxing the plywood subflooring.

Fortunately, at that point, Nijishruljhi declared through a series of eloquent gestures that she intended to find a family who appreciated clean shower heads. It cost me $107.50 to have the carpet relaid.

Finally, I engaged a woman named Griselda, a strapping lass with arms the size of Smithfield hams, who assessed my inadequacies with uncanny accuracy during her first day. The next week she arrived with a stack of *True Confessions* and a bottle of gin, both of which she consumed while I worked, looking up only long enough to raise her feet (which, incidentally, were encased in my bedroom slippers) so that I could vacuum under them.

Six weeks later, after foiling a would-by exhibitionist two blocks from our home (and in the process breaking both his legs and badly mutilating him), Griselda declared our neighborhood to be too risky, and quit.

 *March 1*

I don't know why people bother to name cats. One might as well stand outside at midnight in the rain calling out his street address or phone number as "Here, Muffet." Muffet will only come when she's ready. And she won't be ready until you are in bed with a mustard plaster on your chest.

Of course, when someone yells, "Who ate my alpaca sweater?" you are able to answer, "Muffet," which is not only considerably shorter than "The %°&! cat did," but adds a nice, personal touch.

After six months of observing her apparent satisfaction with Captain Nemo cat food, we bought a sixty-can case of the stuff. We filled every corner of the kitchen with Captain Nemo and had to use the last sixteen cans in the den as bookends and paperweights. That night she took one look at a dish full of Captain Nemo, shuddered, and looked at us as if to say, "Not *this* slop again!"

 March 2

Yesterday we were visited by the tax assessor, who was skulking around from door to door looking for undeclared half bathrooms.

He seemed a bit loath to believe that the only home improvement we had made in the past year was to hang three coat hooks last September, two of which fell off the next day. "I think that I'd better have a look around," he declared skeptically. "What's in there?" he asked, pointing to a closed door with a sign reading KEEP OUT—THIS MEANS YOU.

"That's our daughter's room."

"It looks mighty like a half bathroom to me."

"Well, I don't mind proving it, but maybe you'd better let me go first," I suggested. Entering our daughter's room can be something of risky venture. One can never be completely certain that either something small and furry or something long and slimy has not just gnawed its way out of its cage and isn't at this very moment crouched behind the door preparing to scurry or slither up the leg of the first person to come in.

Obviously, one does not enter such a room without exercising reasonable precautions. As I opened the door, I began flapping my arms and shrieking "Shoo!" at the top of my voice. The caged beasties replied by leaping, panic-stricken, into the air and scattering sawdust onto the already-littered floor.

The tax assessor, who was by now a bit gray around the lips, gave a strangled gasp and pointed to a black object lurking on the desk. I whipped off my shoe and whacked it three time. "It's all right," I said, realizing my error. "It's only a banana peel." It was a foolish mistake; actually our daughter is quite methodical and has a place for everything. Socks go on the study lamp, shoes on her pillow, dirty clothes under the bed, pajamas on the bed post, and banana peels on the desk.

Suppressing a shudder, the tax assessor grabbed his hat and left. He didn't even check to see whether we had converted the broom closet into a half bathroom.

 March 5

I suspect that Supermothers wouldn't dream of sleeping late on Saturday mornings.

If It's Raining

Supermothers probably consider 6:00 A.M. on Saturday an ideal time for creative activities such as baking gingerbread men and teaching their children how to make cunning papier-mache hand puppets out of back issues of *The New Republic*.

I long ago disabused our children of the notion that I would engage in any maternal camaraderie on Saturday mornings before 9:30. I informed them that Daddy and I were to be awakened only in cases of fire, flood, or arterial bleeding. ("Yes, dear, the spurty kind") and that we were *not* to be roused from a sound slumber to be asked what language they speak in Zanzibar, how chickens reproduce, whether they can go to camp next August, or why the elephant painted his toenails red.

I wouldn't want anyone to think that I simply give the children laissez-faire to chop each other's ears off with rusty bread knives or set fire to the piano. Knowing that they wouldn't do anything expressly forbidden, I attempt to anticipate potential trouble by issuing an early morning ultimatum into the darkness. "Don't hit each other with blunt instruments, drink bleach, light matches, or go outside to make a snowman in your pajamas. And if you telephone Grandma long distance, be sure that you reverse the charges."

Unfortunately I am handicapped in that I don't think like a child.

If I had thought like a child last Saturday morning I might have added, "Don't put blue food coloring in your bathwater, Hershey Bars in the toaster, or wash Daddy's sweaters in the dishwasher."

Since I am woefully short on imagination, the children are doomed to spend the rest of their lives light blue from the waist down, the toast tastes like scorched rubber bands, and we now have four men's sweaters, size 6x.

 March 8

I consider myself to be an honest person—except at parties.

The following is a list of remarks (actual meanings are in parentheses), which, when uttered at parties, have caused me to rush to the bathroom mirror and stare at my tongue to be sure it was the same one I had brought in with me.

"I know just what you mean. I was terribly glad to see the Christmas holidays end, too. It's such an exhausting time of year." (We didn't get asked out much, either.)

"Actually, we've had a pretty busy winter. In January we were involved in a sort of archeological dig. You know, unearthing and cataloging ancient artifacts." (We cleaned the basement.)

"Then in February we got terribly caught up in an exciiting artistic project. Experimenting with new techniques is so exhilarating." (We painted the kitchen ceiling. Rather, I painted; my husband held the ladder.)

"Your son is really 'all boy!'" (Isn't it time he was in bed?)

"Yes, my husband is growing a beard. I'm getting to quite like it." (Actually it's exactly like kissing a Brillo Pad, but it does a great job of hiding a double chin.)

"What an attractive dress. Brown is certainly your color." (It makes you look like a walking bratwurst.)

"I know that your daughter would simply love ballet lessons. I do hope that you enroll her in our girl's class." (We desperately need someone else in the car pool.)

"Your dog certainly is playful!" (He just swallowed my watch.)

"You bet I agree that our elementary school is positively medieval in their teaching methods." (Your son must have failed Health Habits, too.)

"We're awfully sorry that we have to leave so early. This migraine hit my husband so suddenly." (Within thirty seconds from the time you brought out the slide projector.)

 March 14

Recently we received a check with the instructions "Buy something that you all will enjoy."

Let's face it, there are precious few things that will appeal to both a forty-year-old and an eleven-year-old, except a steak dinner. Which isn't something that you can dust off and display prominently whenever the giver pops in for a visit.

Games are nice. But the children are hopeless at stud poker. The type of game they enjoy involves negotiating red plastic beans into a pot faster than anyone else. After playing it six times the first evening, we tossed it into the cupboard for six months or so, during which time the dog unearthed it and ate all the beans.

Having been informed by the children that they wouldn't particularly enjoy having a new mailbox, we settled for an outdoor birdfeeder.

We proceeded to fill the feeder with a mixture of suet, hemp, millet, canary seed, oat groats, and egg flake fortified with cod liver oil. The feeder contained everything, in fact, except birds.

During the first two weeks only one bird visited the feeder. He pecked around a bit, made a little gagging noise, and took off again.

Luring the birds became a personal challenge. We tried smorgasbord combination plates of popcorn, rice, Cheerios, and gingersnaps. Finally we hit upon a combination of fruit cocktail and sweet pickle relish.

Birds which normally feed exclusively on crabgrass and caterpillars, as well as others once thought to be extinct, began lining up at dawn and drawing numbers. Some feign broken wings in order to be first in line. If I am late in filling the feeder, they turn surly and begin hammering on the window with their beaks.

Actually we are enjoying the birdfeeder, but a new mailbox wouldn't cost us $3.58 a week for fruit cocktail and sweet pickle relish.

Thanks to our recent acquisition of a birdfeeder, I have taken up bird-watching.

In order to become a serious bird-watcher, it is necessary to obtain a copy of a bird identification book, which features full-color drawings of birds, all doing birdlike things such as building nests, digging worms, and picking lice out of their tails.

Unfortunately for your purposes, these birds are all standing still. Since any birds you will come in contact with will be flashing past at a dizzying rate of speed toward a rendezvous with a picture window, it is necessary to simulate this action by placing the bird book on the floor, covering it with leaves, and running past it as fast as you can.

Birds may be identified by inspecting their eggs, which are colored or speckled, and their beaks, which are small and pointy and ideal for pecking the eyes out of anyone who tries to inspect their eggs.

It is claimed that birds may also be identified by their call. Anything going "tweet-tweet" is most likely a bird. Conversely, birds which go "woof-woof" or "meow" probably aren't.

Many species cannot be distinguished from each other except by obscure markings under their wing-tips or on the bottom of their feet. To add to the confusion, the females of all species are brown.

Since birds take great pains to avoid showing you the bottoms of their feet, one must resort to the technique of bluffing.

If you do succeed in spotting a smallish brown something darting into the eaves, you must declare with conviction "Ah-hah! A Swamp Sparrow." It is possible that someone will have the temerity to say "Are you sure that it wasn't a Vesper Sparrow, Song Sparrow, Fox Sparrow, White-Throated Sparrow, White-Crowned Sparrow or possibly a Robin?"

Simply reply scornfully "Nonsense! Didn't you see the buff-colored patches under his warbles?"

I still can't help but feel that bird-watching is terribly presumptuous, though.

I mean, it's no wonder one has to get up at 5:00 A.M. and trip over all matter of nasty goo while traipsing three miles through the woods in order to try to spot a bird through a pair of high-powered field glasses that are never quite in focus.

The birds are hiding. And I can hardly blame them. What if positions were reversed?

If It's Raining

What if a band of feathered people-watchers descended in great hordes, began pointing their wing-tips at *me* and exclaiming, "Look! There's one now!"

"Where?" the other would retort. "You mean the flat-breasted one with the big tail?"

"That's the one! Notice how drab she is. Obviously the female of the species."

"You're amazing. I can never seem to tell them apart."

"She certainly keeps an untidy nest. Look at all the bits of string, bows from packages, dog-food coupons, and pork chop recipes."

"Disgusting. I understand that she only feeds her young once a day at sundown. It's pitiful watching the fledglings foraging about on their own in the morning, bashing their beaks on the kitchen cabinet doors she's left open."

"Disgusting, yes. But they're awfully interesting to study, actually, especially now that they're on the endangered list. Maybe that's why they're the only species that writes books on their own mating habits."

March 15

One Friday morning, six weeks ago, I was taking a shower and singing a medley of Gershwin hits when my daughter began hammering on the bathroom door.

"Mom!" she bellowed. "The dining room ceiling is leaking like *anything*!"

"Nonsense," I replied, resuming a rudely interrupted chorus of "It Ain't Necessarily So."

Twenty minutes later I sauntered downstairs to find my son sitting under the dining room table, sailing a toy boat.

I called the plumber immediately. "Would someone be home all day?" they asked. Evidently they wanted to make sure that someone was going to be in. Someone *was* in all day, but not the plumber. He arrived promptly at 7:00 A.M. the next morning.

By then Lake Placid was completely dried up.

"Believe me," I said. "It pours like a faucet. Watch." I raced upstairs and turned on both taps. We watched for half an hour. Nothing. I took another shower, sang the same songs. Still nothing.

I wrote the plumber a check for fifteen dollars.

After he left, I turned the shower on again. Water cascaded through the ceiling in sheets. I rushed to phone the plumber.

"It's doing it again!" This time he arrived in half an hour. By then the leak had stopped.

"But you can *see* the water on the floor."

"Maybe you spilled something," he suggested skeptically. "Maybe the kids did it. What about the dog? Lady, I fix leaks, not puddles."

I wrote out another check for fifteen dollars.

This poignant drama has been going on for six weeks. The plumber has torn up the bathroom floor, only to find it dry and dusty underneath. Yesterday, however, he finally came up with a solution.

"Lady," he said. "If I were you, I'd move."

☂ *March 18*

I knew that my son was really ill when he passed up supper.

"But it's fried chicken!" I pointed out, waving a drumstick tantalizingly under his nose.

"My stomach hurts," Eric replied.

"He just wants to get out of walking the dog," was his sister's unsympathetic reaction.

For the past ten years I have viewed every pain occurring below the Adam's apple and above the knees as possible appendicitis. Seventeen appendicitis attacks have turned out to be stomach flu. Twenty-four have been constipation. One was a fractured pelvis.

I began gently prodding Eric's stomach.

"Cut that out!" he snarled.

"I'm looking for McBurney's Point."

"Who is McBurney, and what is his point doing in my stomach?"

"McBurney's point is a place between your hip bone and your bellybutton." As an aside to my daughter, I added, "If he screams when I poke it, he has appendicitis. If he laughs, he's just trying to get out of walking the dog."

"Yahgah!" bleated Eric as I located McBurney's point.

"By George, I think he's got it!" I gasped. Within twenty minutes we were sitting in the emergency ward of the hospital, where Eric reluctantly parted with several specimens of various bodily fluids and had his McBurney's Point ruthlessly prodded by two surgeons, three residents, and an inquisitive orderly. They disappeared for three hours, leaving us to watch the admissions of three automobile accidents, two drug overdoses, and a drunk with a broken nose. Meanwhile, Eric's appendix whiled away the time by flopping around like a dying mackerel.

By 2:00 A.M. the doctors announced that Eric and his appendix should part company immediately. I kissed Eric on the cheek as he was being wheeled into surgery.

"You shouldn't do that," he warned. "You'll catch appendicitis."

"Are you sure that he's all right?" I asked the surgeon after the operation.

"All right!" he laughed. "He isn't even out of the recovery room yet and he's asking whether we have any fried chicken."

Eric was keenly disappointed when the surgeon refused to give him his appendix, as he had planned to put it under his pillow for the appendix fairy, reasoning that if baby teeth were worth twenty-five cents each, an appendix could bring at least $7.50.

The appendix was next to have been featured in a Show and-Tell presentation at school, then bronzed for his grandmother to use as a paperweight.

Eric shares a hospital room in the children's ward with another appendectomy, a case of colitis, and a rash of undetermined origin whose owner assured me isn't the least bit contagious—probably.

The boys spend their days checking the drip flow on each other's intravenous feeding bottles, swapping "why-did-the-elephant" jokes, and shooting rubber bands at the nurse's aides.

The day following his operation, Eric received four jigsaw puzzles, twelve comic books, twenty-seven greeting cards, and three hamburgers for lunch. Whereupon he announced that he was in no particular hurry to return home.

"They let me stay up till 10:00," he announced. "And we don't have to take baths," he added significantly, turning on the TV to watch a "Gilligan's Island" rerun.

By the next day, Eric had completed the four jigsaw puzzles, read all twelve comic books twice, and lunched on creamed spinach and carrot sticks.

"I kind of miss being home and going to school," he conceded, handing me a soggy napkin full of creamed spinach. "Especially since I have something for Show-and-Tell."

"Swell. What is it?"

"Billy's rash."

Since hospitals are inhabited solely by the Afflicted and the Healers, a visitor is clearly a misfit, looking neither sick enough to be a patient nor clean enough to be a nurse.

Feeling as welcome as a blizzard in May, I visited a friend Myra while checking on Eric. I found her sharing a room with a thin, blonde woman with a faint, black moustache who was scrutinizing her tongue in a hand mirror. Myra seemed a bit uncertain whether hospital protocol demanded that she introduce me.

"I'd like you to meet Mrs. Berger," she finally said.

"Colitis," announced Mrs. Berger, wrenching her attention away from her tongue.

"I beg your pardon?"

"Colitis," she repeated. "You wouldn't believe the misery I'm in." The three of us observed thirty seconds of silence in wordless homage to Mrs. Berger's unbelievable colitis.

"Don't she look terrible?" demanded Mrs. Berger, pointing accusingly at Myra. I had to admit that I had seen Myra look better, but lying in bed for four days watching your toenails grow isn't exactly calculated to put roses in your cheeks.

I groped for an opening gambit. It seemed somewhat pointless to say "How are you?" to anyone with twenty-seven stitches in her stomach. "How do you feel?" while a bit more appropriate, was likely to elicit a lengthy and somewhat nauseatingly graphic reply.

"How are the meals?" I asked at last.

"Terrible. But everyone has to eat them eventually. On Monday they give you a broiled chicken back. If you don't eat it, the next day they chop it up with canned peas and make chicken salad. If you still won't eat it, Mrs. Berger says that they puree it and inject it into your hip.

"Thanks for the flowers," she said, vaguely indicating a table full of vases. Since I had ordered them by phone I had no idea which ones were mine. I tried to determine which bunch looked most like $2.75. It certainly couldn't be the three dozen longstemmed roses. I fervently hoped that mine wasn't the single lily in the water glass.

Just then the nurse announced that since it was time for dinner, I would have to leave. "Unless you'd like to stay," she said, waving a hypodermic needle. "We're having a lovely puree of chicken."

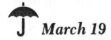 *March 19*

Last week my daughter approached me indignantly.

"Do you realize that I am the only girl in my entire class

who still wears those crummy Fruit of the Loom undershirts? I want a bra. A training bra."

"Training for *what!*" I demanded.

"Don't be crude. Here in the mail-order catalog it says that training bras 'provide gentle support for the blossoming girl as she prepares to flower into womanhood.' I'm blossoming, in case you haven't noticed."

"My little girl!" I sobbed, clasping her tightly to me. "Are you *sure* you're blossoming? I mean, you seem pretty much like you always were to me."

She favored me with a huffy stare and stalked off to her room.

The next afternoon we visited the lingerie department of the local department store.

"Now, *that's* what I want," she announced, pointing to a display of purple lace bras with matching bikini panties.

"That's what is known as sending a man on a boy's errand," I informed her.

"May I help you ladies?" a salesgirl inquired. My daughter flung me a "So There!" glance.

"I need a new bra," she declared. "I don't exactly have a favorite brand," she added, gathering up fifteen assorted makes and sizes and heading for the fitting room.

The next morning my daughter appeared decidedly depressed at breakfast.

"It's tight," she complained.

"It's supposed to be tight."

"The straps cut into my shoulders."

"The straps are supposed to cut into your shoulders."

"Does it show through the back of my blouse?"

"Don't worry. You can't see a thing."

"Darn it. I'll have to change to a thinner blouse. What's the good of wearing a bra unless people can see it? You might as well wear an undershirt."

Who's to blame for this early interest in wearing a bra? Not me, that's for sure. It must be the constant barrage of advertisements.

Now I am sure that there is a valid need for such advertise-

If It's Raining

ments. (Actually, I'm not all *that* sure, but it seems appropriate to try to be positive.)

What I can't seem to understand is why underwear models, without exception, appear to be gripped in the throes of some unexplained passion. Evidently it is considered bad form to simply stand around in a Playtex bra, casually inspecting your fingernails; convention obviously insists that you must assume sultry expressions, thrust both arms upward in lascivious abandon, and fling locks of hair wantonly over both eyes, presumably leaving no doubt in the mind of the prospective purchaser that being encased in a Playtex bra is an erotic event.

The most intriguing advertisement of all is the "before and after" approach, featuring a hapless matron, her midriff bulging alarmingly and her posterior shaped like a brace of enormous butternut squash. The second view features the same matron wearing a girdle which has not only rendered her midriff and posterior svelte and smooth, but has inexplicably removed the circles from under her eyes, obliterated the gray from her hair, and capped her front teeth.

Ironically, no such miraculous transformation of libido and shape is hinted at by those who model men's underwear.

Invariably they are pictured either sitting sheepishly around a locker room, shaking foot powder into their executive-length socks, or with one foot propped on a bench, staring grimly at the camera, obviously tormented by the crucial decision of whether to finish getting dressed or simply go back to bed.

 *March 20*

Not only do many couples consider a double bed to be an ideal arena in which to resolve major conflicts, such as whether or not permanent-press handkerchiefs want ironing, but they bring to the arena two combatants with wildly divergent body temperatures—it being a proven fact that by 2:00 A.M. the female body temperature plummets to 89 degrees while that of the male shoots up to 112.5.

Consequently, a typical wife insists upon covering up her husband all night, reasoning that if she is cold, he must be too.

Her husband, in turn, spends the greater part of every night with beads of sweat coating his upper lip, dreaming that he has been staked out on the Sahara Desert at high noon as a penalty for not taking out the garbage.

In the throes of his discomfort, he occasionally succeeds in flinging his half of the covers over his sleeping wife, while whimpering "But the bag wasn't *full!*" Finally comfortable, he drifts off into a deep sleep, dreaming that he is swinging lazily on a hammock, deep in a cool forest glen, while six maidens hover nearby, ironing his handkerchiefs.

March 22

I must admit to being decidedly underimpressed with artsy-craftsy projects.

I have found that no matter how many red sequins you glue on them, bleach bottles still look inordinately like bleach bottles.

Pipe cleaners don't exactly set my artistic libido atwitter, nor do used S.O.S. Pads, empty orange juice cans, or the cardboard tubes from toilet paper rolls.

To my way of thinking, there is nothing remotely festive about a Christmas wreath made out of green garbage bags and a bent coat hanger.

Once, stricken with an acute attack of conscience over the ecological problems of our society, I went so far as to buy a bottle-cutter set which promised to enable me to make glasses out of those ten cases of empty beer bottles in the basement. I discovered that one case of beer makes more glasses than I'll ever need; instead of a basement full of ten cases of empty beer bottles, I ended up with a basement full of 240 ugly brown glasses.

Unfortunately, I happen to live in an area of compulsive driftwood collectors.

"You're *not* going to throw away grapefruit rinds!?!" shrieked one of my neighbors, carrying on as if she'd just caught me rinsing my hair with Holy Water.

"What's wrong with throwing away a grapefruit rind?"

"You *save* it," she insisted, rinsing off the coffee grounds and carefully patting it dry. "Orange peels, apple parings—it all makes heavenly sachet."

Thanks to diligent hoarding, I now have seventeen little bags of garbage hanging in my closet.

Not only does everything I own smell like a fruit salad that sat out in the sun too long, but I draw flies.

March 24

There is something regenerative about the approach of spring. As the doldrums of winter begin to lift, I find myself seeking to rejuvenate my life, to cleanse my soul and greet the awakening of nature with a spirit of unadulterated purity and innocence.

I accomplish this by having a garage sale.

This year I resolve to be absolutely ruthless, there being no room for sentiment in an eight-by-ten storage room. While I intend to keep the four ping-pong paddles I found beside the washing machine in hopes that we get a table some day, I see no justification for keeping a repair kit for an air mattress that I left in Yosemite National Park in 1972.

And while I have no intention of having another baby, if one came to visit I should probably be quite glad to have a wooden gate or two to keep between us.

While there is no possible way I could be induced to part with a crepe paper daisy costume from the second-grade production of "Bluebird Hill," a beer bottle covered with gold-sprayed macaroni shells, or a jewelry box full of the dog's baby teeth, the following items are definitely for sale:

Fourteen gallon cider jugs with strands of green mold inside.

One 1970 Denver, Colorado, phone book.

A sleeping bag that smells funny and has a jammed zipper.

One potty chair bearing the original price tag. Never used.

A jigsaw puzzle entitled "Aristotle Contemplating the Bust of Raquel Welch," with six pieces missing.

One bird cage, one hamster cage, one aquarium, one turtle bowl, a cat's scratching post, a rabbit hutch, three bags of cedar shavings, and a shoe box with holes punched in the lid.

Of course, along with the garage sale, spring also brings with it another primordial urge. And, overcome with the same inexplicable urge that sends salmon upstream to spawn, I know that I will come dangerously close to cleaning the house.

I don't mean simple "wipe-the-jelly-off-the-commode" type cleaning.

I mean real cleaning. Putting Spic and Span on a toothbrush and scrubbing all the little knobs on the stove. Taking the TV set apart and dusting the tubes. Waxing the garage floor.

For anyone who comes close to pandering to this primordial urge, I recommend asking the following questions:

1. In these critical days of world crisis and economic upheaval, can you in all conscience devote an entire day to rearranging your spice rack?

2. In the final analysis, will anyone really care whether the grout around your bathtub is gray?

3. Can you really leave this world knowing that your only contribution to global harmony is having a spotless broiler pan?

4. The last time you indulged in such an orgy of cleanli-

ness, you gave birth two hours later. Granted, there may not be a causal relationship, but do you really want to take that chance?

 **March 25**

Any mother with children at home who attempts to enjoy a short telephone conversation finds her attention constantly diverted by horrendous thumping noises, rather like someone throwing a cat down a laundry chute, followed by the less-than-reassuring exclamation "Boy! Are *you* gonna get it!"

If at this point she does not get up, the thumping will stop, unfortunately being replaced by a repetitious sound, vaguely reminiscent of the cry of an indignant moose, which indicates that someone is using his bed as a trampoline.

This temporary diversion soon gives way to the authoritative sound of nailing, pounding and/or sawing, as the children peremptorily decide to add or subtract a spare bedroom.

Actually, the most frightening sound of all is total silence, indicating that someone is either painting his shoes, cutting out all the pictures in the *Encyclopedia Britannica* to send to Grandma, or drinking an entire bottle of Mr. Clean.

March 26

At one time, I thought that it was a perfectly splendid idea for my son to have a paper route.

Wanting a paper route, I believed, exhibited an admirable

desire to assume responsibility and would lead to a much needed appreciation for the value of money.

It also meant that I wouldn't have to raise his allowance this year.

I must admit that a paper route has, in fact, increased his sense of responsibility. As he feels an obligation to attend to his regular customers first, we now receive the last paper, the one that fell in the puddle and has the sports section missing.

A paper route has improved his regard for the value of money, too. Where once he was so unconcerned about money that I regularly would retrieve on the average of eighty-eight cents in change from the lint filter whenever I washed his jeans, now he refuses to deliver a paper to me unless he is paid in advance. And unless I tip him, he throws it on the roof. When anyone asks what he wants to be when he grows up, he replies "a tycoon."

In return for this semireliable service, I occasionally help him out when he is ill, has a detention, is practicing his trumpet, or has a blister on his heel. While he can lob a newspaper twenty-five feet directly onto the center of a welcome mat, the only direction I can throw is straight up. So far, I have heaved seventeen papers into trees, thirty-two onto roofs, and have witnessed four disappear completely.

This I don't mind. What I do not enjoy is collecting for him.

"You're not Eric!" one man said accusingly. Before I could explain coyly that he should notice a family resemblance, he marched off to the kitchen and said, "There's a new paperboy out there come to collect, Emma. Big gawky kind of kid. I just don't know what this younger generation's coming to; I could swear he was wearing curlers!"

March 29

I am not certain at just what age a birthday ceases to be a Joyous Occasion.

If It's Raining

I do know that the period between "now I am old enough to" and "now I am too old to" is frighteningly short.

I find that these days, birthdays are less a question of doing something special than of remembering how to do everyday things. And wondering whether they're worth the bother.

"Why didn't you tell us that today was your birthday?" the children demanded recently.

"I forgot that it *was* my birthday," I admitted.

"But we could have had a party," they protested.

"I would sooner celebrate the Saint Valentine's Day Massacre. At my age, parties are in bad taste—kind of like setting off Roman Candles to celebrate the invasion of Pearl Harbor."

"Just think of all the neat presents you missed getting."

"Who needs six more flannel nightgowns?" I scoffed.

"Somehow I never thought you would be the type to be sensitive about getting older," mused my daughter. "Next you'll be telling us that you lie about your age."

"Of course I lie about my age," I retorted. "I tell everyone that I'm sixty-two."

"Whatever for? You could pass for thirty!"

"Think about it," I replied. "Which would you rather be known as, a dissipated thirty, or a remarkably well-preserved sixty-two?"

 March 30

"I just can't understand you, Millie," I protested to my friend last week as we slid into her car. "You just don't seem like the type for a CB radio."

"Nonsense," countered Millie. "A CB radio enables me to add my voice to those of my fellow men, Sweet Baby, Dirty

Dan, and Big Foot. Together we sing the song of the open road. Or we will as soon as I learn the jargon."

"Super Stud calling those pretty little beavers in the pregnant roller skate," bawled the radio. "If you're making for Sugar Town on a big 10-17, I'd be more than happy to cover your rear."

"Just what does he mean by that?" hissed Millie, clutching the steering wheel grimly and peering nervously into the rear view mirror.

"I think Super Stud is either that orange van with the baby shoes hanging over the dashboard or the purple pick-up truck we passed that had the 'Honk If You Love Jesus' bumper sticker. He wants you to join him in singing the song of the open road. Or something."

"I don't care what you say," Millie insisted. "If my car breaks down now, I can use my CB instead of that 38-D bra I used to tie to the antenna as a distress flag."

"But you don't wear a 38-D bra."

"How much help do your think I would have gotten waving a Fruit of the Loom undershirt?"

April 2

Reading in bed is an art.

One must first choose the proper bed. A single bed is rarely wide enough to accommodate a sufficient number of pillows, not to mention a box of Kleenex, an ashtray, a plate of Things to Nibble On, and a second book to read in case you decide you don't like the first one.

A double bed is better, unless you must share it with someone who flops around and makes exasperated noises while you're trying to read.

Choosing appropriate food to eat in bed is a problem. One should avoid anything with seeds, as they invariably mix themselves up with the bedding and leave you with nasty looking marks on your cheeks the next morning. Although crumbs can be annoying, it is relatively simple to mop them up by dabbing at the sheets with a piece of bread covered with peanut butter.

Pajamas are a nice touch when one is reading in bed. They not only speak of elegance and refinement, but keep the crumbs off one's chest. Bottoms should be roomy enough so that one can slide down in bed without hurting oneself.

The book should be something light and entertaining, as it is patently ridiculous to make such elaborate preparations, only to fall asleep on page two of *Agriculture in the Middle Ages.*

April 3

Since we had children, I've discovered that housework is never really finished. At some point it becomes necessary simply to declare, "There now, that's entirely enough of *that!*" or you'll find yourself at 4:30 in the afternoon waxing the underside of the coffee table and sobbing.

As it is, after spending eighteen hours washing windows, sweeping floors, and scrubbing peanut butter off the TV screen, I fall into bed with a sense of accomplishment. Whereupon a still, small voice begins to whine, "Yeah, smarty, but what about all the toast crumbs in the silverware drawer?"

A friend of mine insists that all I need is a system, like her Room-a-Day method. On Monday, she cleans the living room; on Tuesday, the family room—and so on. Unfortunately, when I tried her system, the living room that I cleaned on Monday was not only full of old boots and Oh Henry! wrappers again on Wednesday, but I found that someone had traced a decidedly vulgar word in the dust on the stereo.

I'm not certain where kitchens fit in this one-a-day scheme. It's all very well to declare Thursday as "clean-the-kitchen" day, but what happens when the Sunday dinner ham shoots off the platter, slides the length of the kitchen, and bounces down the back stairs? I suppose that in theory one could refuse to deal with the twenty-foot smear of ham fat on the floor, it not being Thursday and all.

But unless one is willing to risk having a husband, two children, and the TV repairman bouncing down the back stairs as well, it becomes necessary to maintain a three-day vigil in the kitchen, cautioning, "Hop over the ham fat, dear" to everyone.

I prefer my "If-I-don't-see-it-nobody-else-will-either" attitude. But every system has its drawback. Yesterday I saw our son Eric and his friend down on their hands and knees, peering under Eric's bed. "Wow! You win!" declared the friend, and handed Eric fifteen cents.

If It's Raining

"What was that all about?" I asked Eric later.

"Oh, I just bet Murray fifteen cents that I had more dust under my bed than he had under his."

 April 10

I recently ran across a magazine article entitled "Ten House Plants Which ANYONE Can Grow."

If one is addicted to absurd hyperbole, this article ranks a close second behind the lead story, "How to Look Adorable When You're Eight Months Pregnant."

In the first place, the writer was adamant in insisting that plants need to be placed in an area of the house where they will receive sufficient light. Unfortunately, I have only one such area, and it is presently occupied by the refrigerator. Where I desperately need a plant is in the darkest corner of the living room beside the heat vent.

"Overwatering," contended the writer, "is probably the most common problem affecting would-be gardeners. Overwatering causes the plant's leaves to drop off." As the leaves are likewise prone to drop off when the plant is underwatered, overfertilized, or afflicted with mealy worms, one can never be completely certain where one went wrong should the plant suddenly fall into the kitchen sink and lie there looking up balefully through the egg shells and coffee grounds.

"Try talking to your plants," urged the author in conclusion. "They'll love you for it."

Regrettably, he neglected to suggest suitable topics of conversation. Let's face it, an African Violet is verging on being inanimate; how can one discuss the problem of urban decay with something doomed to spend its entire life in a six-inch plastic pot?

I find that reading material on raising houseplants is much

like reading the final chapters of *The Joy of Sex*; I know that thousands of people can follow the fairly involved directions and experience unqualified success and enjoyment, but can I? And even if I could, do I really want to?

It's not that I haven't tried.

I have a philodendron located on a window sill, carefully out of direct sunlight, which I regularly ply with the very best fertilizer and seventy-eight-degree distilled water. I protect it from drafts, loud noises, and rude language. We not only sit down for daily chats, but I play classical music to it and read it inspirational verse every Tuesday. Its only response is to sit there clasping its terminal bud dramatically, wheezing, and dropping leaves into the kitchen sink.

I called on my next-door neighbor yesterday only to find her practically lashed to the piano with tendrils of English ivy. While I watched, not only did three leaves unfold and six buds appear, but I could swear the entire plant was humming "Happy Days Are Here Again" in close harmony.

"Stop that, you little devil," she chortled, absently unwrapping a tendril that had entwined itself around her neck and was nibbling her earlobe amorously.

"Isn't it the oddest thing?" she exclaimed. "I simply never remember to feed or water it. I can't understand how it stays alive."

"You must do *something*," I argued. "Your plant is so healthy it's almost embarrassing to watch!"

"Well, I do read to it," she admitted.

"Inspirational verse?"

"No," she blushed. "*The Joy of Sex*."

Something larger than houseplants looms before me now, however, and that is the outdoor garden. The two momentous decisions facing me (and every homeowner) this month are: (1) What to plant, (2) What to plant it with.

The first problem is more easily solved if you either lean heavily toward the practicality of cucumbers or vibrate whenever you spy a petunia. Unfortunately I tend to vacillate. I mean, petunias taste revolting, yet cucumbers won't fit in a bud vase.

One must also consider things like soil acidity, drainage, and exposure to the sun, a thorough study of which can stretch well into July, nicely solving the problem, as by then it is too late to plant anything but radishes.

Once you have determined what to plant, the next pressing problem lies in locating the proper tools. In my case, intense questioning administered under an extremely hot light elicited the information that the trowel had been used to fix a bicycle.

"How can you fix a bicycle with a trowel?" I wailed.

"You can't."

Muttering obscenities, I strode into the garden with sixteen packages of seeds and a tablespoon.

The package directions specified that the seeds be planted as early in the spring as the soil can be worked. It is extremely difficult to work soil with a nine-inch tablespoon. It involved getting down on my hands and knees and stabbing away at a clump of clay only to discover that, since the clump was in reality a beef knuckle bone that the dog buried last fall, the attendant vibrations loosened all the fillings in my molars.

Now seed packet illustrations should undoubtedly be given "The Most Blatant Example of False Advertising Award."

If only seed companies would feature color illustrations of green beans covered with slugs, cucumbers riddled with worm holes, and cabbages being engulfed by a slimy, reddish-brown fungus, one would at least be partially prepared for the inevitable.

Instead, seed companies insist upon presenting breathtakingly gorgeous, full-color views of a virgin tomato, unblemished save for a drop of morning dew clinging to its flawless stem, a pea pod bursting open spontaneously to reveal twelve perfectly matched peas, and a head of lacy lettuce coyly uncurling in the summer sun.

Those of us even remotely susceptible to the "Mary Mary Quite Contrary" syndrome inevitably go all to pieces in the face of such bounty.

I mean, if it all hadn't looked so gorgeous, I never would

have forgotten that our entire garden plot consists of a six-by-six feet area beside the garbage cans when I snatched up twenty-seven packets of assorted vegetables that no one in the family likes anyway.

Eventually I reached the stage where I arbitrarily declared the soil to be ready.

But it was something of a shock to open the seed packages and discovered that the next step involved planting what appeared to be several thousand grains of pepper individually.

At that point it seemed infinitely more logical to simply rebury the bone.

"What did you plant in the garden?" my son asked.

"A cow," I replied. "And if it ever comes up, I sure have a lot of pepper to put on the steaks."

 *April 14*

I am a firm believer in getting away from the children periodically.

Not only is a brief hiatus from sharing a common bathroom beneficial to all concerned, but a short separation from mother causes the children to appreciate her exceptional care and tenderness which heretofore they have taken for granted.

On the other hand, there is always the possibility that they will realize that they are not only perfectly capable of managing without you, but prefer it that way, and will answer your long-distance phone calls with "Mother who?"

Of course, one cannot simply pack a bag and slip away silently into the night, no matter how attractive the prospect may appear after an entire evening of watching them spit in each other's milk.

No, you must, in all conscience, recruit a caretaker to sleep in your bed till 10:00 every morning, watch "The Edge of Night," thaw the TV dinners, and otherwise function as you would.

One cannot turn such heady responsibility over to a stranger without first briefing her on family routine, personal idiosyncrasies, and the fact that there is a garter snake named Arthur loose in the house.

Consequently, I am leaving the following note for the sitter:

Dear Mildred:
It is Eric's turn to stomp on the Fruit Loops box so that it will fit in the garbage bag, and Laurie's turn to use the plunger on the kitchen sink.

The stuff in the green refrigerator jar is Hamburger Surprise; the dog food is in the pink refrigerator jar. Don't get them mixed up. The dog hates Hamburger Surprise.

The sugar is in the canister marked flour; the flour is in "Sugar." The one labeled "Coffee" has a bottle of cooking sherry inside; it's a little salty, but not too bad if you drink it fast.

As there is always the possibility that a parent who goes away from the children for a weekend of adult-type revelry may meet with some sort of fatal disaster, whenever I go away I take great pains to leave my dresser drawers in immaculate condition, ensuring that any concerned neighbors who begin rummaging through my personal effects searching for insurance policies and stock certificates will be impressed with my housekeeping skills.

I have likewise taken the precaution of tucking the following letter to the children under a pile of panty hose:

Dear Children:
I'm sorry that I'm not able to leave you much money. There would have been a lot more if your teeth had come in straight.

This Must Be the Weekend   57

There is, however, a college fund set aside for you to use at any college you choose that doesn't have coeducational dormitories.

I want you to know that I loved you when you flushed your new shoes down the toilet, shaved your eyebrows off, and wrapped the dead sparrow in waxed paper, labeled him "Pork Chops," and put him in the freezer. It was probably hard for you to realize that I loved you, what with me going all white around the mouth and screaming "If you *ever* do that again, I'm going to *belt* you!"

But if I *didn't* love you, I wouldn't have cared.

I mean, you may not grow up to become presidents of the United States or nuclear physicists, but at least you won't grow up to be the kind of adults who go around pouring their Ovaltine down heat vents.

Love,
Mom

P.S. Better buy more dental floss; I used the last of it to tie up my suitcase.

 *April 16*

While dinner should be an occasion of family harmony, all too often the evening meal is fraught with dissent.

What is clearly needed is the following "Code of Behavior at Mealtime," a copy of which should be conspicuously posted in the dining room.

Cleanliness: Children are required to wash all visible moving parts, i.e., hands, faces, ears. There is nothing quite so revolting as eating opposite someone with a Chiquita Banana label on his forehead or "I Love Rod Stewart" written on her hand in green ballpoint ink.

If It's Raining

Food: Any comments on the quantity or quality of the food are restricted to those of an affirmative nature. Rhetorical questions such as "Why do we always have to have crummy old beets?" are detrimental to morale. Food is to be consumed as quickly as is politely possible, using only the utensils provided, i.e., there will be no manual arrangement of peas to spell "I Love Rod Stewart."

Physical Restrictions: Tipping chairs is positively disallowed, as are intricate balancing acts involving glasses of milk. Elbows and knees are to be kept off the table.

Conversation: Each member of the family may choose one topic and browbeat it for three minutes. Son may use his three minutes to describe how to make an amplifier. Daughter may explain how she is going to take a paper route to earn enough money to send for a Mark Eden Bust Developer. Mother may muse aloud on the difficulty of removing carbonized chicken pie from the inside of an oven. Father will use his three minutes for silence. Any topic is allowed, with the exception of those discussions beginning "Guess what I saw on the sidewalk on the way to school!"

 *April 19*

Don't get me wrong. I think that pantyhose are possibly the greatest invention since sliced bread.

In theory pantyhose are the answer. But why can I never find a pair that fits?

I am either forced to spend the entire day encased in a pair of pantyhose so large that even though I pull them up to my armpits, my ankles and knees are festooned with wrinkles, or I must attempt to wedge into a smaller size which never goes quite all the way on.

And it is most distressing to walk down the street with the

elastic top clinging precariously to my hip bones, the crotch in the general vicinity of my knees, and the uneasy realization that any ill-considered physical activity will undoubtedly cause the entire effort to snap down around my ankles.

J *April 21*

"You really should jog," a friend of mine declared recently.

"Whatever for?" I shuddered.

"It's such good exercise!" she crowed. Actually, as reasons go, good exercise does not exactly set me all a-flutter. I mean, it's not as if she said that jogging tasted good or paid $28.50 an hour.

Besides, I tried jogging two years ago.

The first morning I ventured out in a pair of emerald green stretch pants and a snappy red hockey shirt that my son had bought at the Salvation Army for fifty-five cents. Evidently this garb did not immediately identify me as a jogger. Not only did four buses stop to pick me up, but it took me fifteen minutes to convince a cruising member of the vice squad that I wasn't being pursued by a sex maniac.

I tried again a week later, this time wearing not only a blue track suit but a sweatband around my forehead and a shirt cardboard bearing the number "27" taped to my back.

I was doing quite well until I was joined by a German Shepherd who seemed good-naturedly determined to hamstring me. He gamboled along beside me, slathering coyly, alternately licking my hand and making slashing motions at my ankles.

"Good boy!" I bleated. Obviously offended at this blatant bit of hypocrisy, Good Boy lunged for my throat. A burst of speed fortunately rendered this area out of reach, although

If It's Raining

he managed to snatch and eat my shirt cardboard.

This permanently retired both me and my number from jogging. At least until it starts paying $28.50 an hour.

 April 22

While I was never particularly enchanted with the prospect of hauling an orange-and-white striped teddy bear, two dozen baby bottles, and a rubber sheet half way across the country, I've discovered that traveling with small children is a lead-pipe cinch compared with taking two children on a three thousand-mile trip to California.

In the first place, my son Eric insisted on packing his own clothes in a fourteenth-hand duffel bag that he bought for twenty-five cents at a Navy surplus store and arrived in California with six pairs of shoes, an electric blow comb, and twelve copies of *Mad* magazine.

"What do you mean, you 'forgot' underwear?" I demanded.

"I remembered to bring socks," he countered.

"Yeah. One green and one blue," I sighed.

"Where's my room?" his sister, Laurie inquired.

"You're standing in it."

"We're not all sharing one room!?! You mean I have to sleep in the same room with 'It?'" she wailed, gesturing toward her brother.

"Yuck!" Eric grimaced, indicating that he too was somewhat less than overjoyed at the prospect.

"Think of this room as our home away from home," I insisted. Within ten minutes they had draped their jeans over the chairs, slung underwear over the lamps, and taped three posters up on the walls.

"This place is as much a mess as your rooms at home," I

complained. "I hope you're comfortable now."

"As comfortable as a growing boy can be without a refrigerator," Eric grumbled.

"And the phone," Laurie added. "I've been here for twenty minutes, and it hasn't rung *once*."

While on such a trip, one is happily freed from the onerous chore of meal preparation. The resulting euphoria is more than a little offset by having to take children to break bread, not to mention an odd dish or two, in restaurants.

As I discovered in California, a 7:00 A.M. breakfast is a hands-down favorite as the worst possible meal to eat outside the home.

While within the confines of familiar surroundings, a mother can shuffle aimlessly about the kitchen wearing a chin strap and clutching a cup of coffee, ricochet gently from the refrigerator to the stove, wondering idly where the toaster has got to. In the face of such amiable helplessness, the children may very well realize that she definitely is in no shape to be trusted with a bread knife and decide to fix their own breakfasts.

"You have blue eye shadow all over your ear," my daughter Laurie hissed as we entered a coffee shop in California.

"I *thought* my eyelids seemed bumpier than usual," I sighed.

"Am I ever *starved!*" my son Eric confided to our waitress, a motherly-looking woman wearing black fishnet stockings and a pink micro-miniskirt.

"Isn't he *cute!*" gushed the waitress, mentally computing fifteen percent of a $12.50 breakfast order.

"I'll have the Lumberjack's Special, with a double order of sausage, four English muffins, a bowl of Fruit Loops, and two large glasses of orange juice," Eric announced. "For starters."

"And I'll have a cheese and bacon omelette, hash-browned potatoes, cream of wheat, a Danish pastry, and tomato juice," Laurie said. "What are you having, Mom?"

"Black coffee and a glass of prune juice."

"It sure is embarrassing to eat breakfast in a restaurant

If It's Raining

with you," Laurie whispered.

"Lots of people drink prune juice," I replied huffily

"Yeah. But not while they're wearing a chin strap."

 April 23

The fantasy of Disneyland comes as no real shock to anyone who has already spent several days in southern California.

During those first necessary days, one loses the initial mistrust of California foliage, which is of the same bizarre, exotic quality which Northerners only encounter as decorations in third-class restaurants, as well as the uncomfortable certainty that on the underside of every leaf are the words "Made in Japan."

It is also necessary, as a prelude to Disneyland, to have made frequent stops at drive-in restaurants and experienced the ridiculous self-consciousness of having to recite your order to a large plastic clown.

Disneyland is composed of forty-two attractions, the lines for many of which were long, doubling back on themselves snake-fashion five and six times. The barriers which are erected to prevent interlopers from breaking into line are equally effective in keeping anyone already queued up from changing his mind and heading for a free exhibit instead.

Through sheer strength of numbers, the children forced me into a Matterhorn bobsled, which wound its way through a man-made mountain at a dizzying rate.

"I wish you wouldn't scream that way," my son observed.

"It's the only way I know!" I howled before lapsing into a moan-sob combination which lasted until we careened back down the Matterhorn.

While, with the exception of the Matterhorn disaster, I enjoyed Disneyland, I was evidently not the only one struck by

This Must Be the Weekend

Disneyland's pervading unreality, which extends even to its restrooms. I watched a six-year-old boy, obviously distraught, rush back to where his mother stood waiting.

"Quick! Quick!" he bellowed. "Am I a 'Prince' or a 'Princess'?"

 April 25

It has often been said that the best part of traveling is coming home again.

This is not necessarily true.

This is especially not necessarily true when one is returning home in the company of two children who have spent an entire week combing southern California beaches for "souvenirs," which, more often than not, turn out to be recently-deceased marine life.

"You smell funny!" I whispered to my daughter as we waited to go through the airport security check.

"It's not me," she declared. "It's my starfish. I bet I'll be the only one on the entire plane with a starfish."

"You'll probably be the only one on the entire plane—period!" I gasped, struggling to move upwind of the pungent bulge in her jean jacket.

"Where are your socks?" I asked, noticing that she wore none.

"They're in my suitcase. I have clams in one, dead hermit crabs in another, some weird sort of black, slimy thing with six legs in . . . "

"What in heaven's name are you going to do with that stuff?"

"Give it all to Jane," she replied. "To show her I was thinking about her."

"I can see it all now," I said sarcastically. "Here's a black, slimy thing with six legs, Jane. When I saw it, I immediately thought of you."

"Jane will think it's cool," she maintained stubbornly.

"You don't have any souvenirs in *your* socks, do you?" I asked my son.

"I didn't bring any socks, remember?"

As it turned out, he did bring home a souvenir. A perfectly spectacular, absolutely authentic case of athlete's foot.

May 6

I am not particularly fond of animal acts. Rather than watching a bear in red velvet knickers ride a motorcycle, I would much prefer to see him out in the wild, doing something that nature intended him to do. Like raiding garbage dumps.

Over the protests of the children, I have vetoed their attempts to teach our dogs to do any of the following tricks:

Shake Hands: While I've never been accused of being a fanatic on hygiene, I'm not particularly enchanted with the prospect of shaking hands with anyone who spends the entire day tromping through freshly fertilized tulip beds and spilled orange juice.

Beg: I'm not sure what other people feed their dogs, but I'd be embarrassed to suggest to our dog that he beg for the revolting muck that we put into his dish. It's terribly good for him and all, but he greets every meal with a resigned sigh and holds his nose with one paw while he eats.

Speak: I've never heard of a dog saying anything constructive, or even remotely entertaining. When you teach a dog to speak, you teach him to bark, which is precisely the same thing that you bashed him with a rolled-up newspaper for doing just yesterday.

Besides, with one child launching into a lengthy diatribe on the impossibility of functioning in an inflationary consumer-oriented society on an allowance of $1.50 a month, the other

If It's Raining

child complaining that he's the only boy in the whole school who has to carry a pink lunchbox with a picture of Cinderella on it, and a husband wistfully asking where all his clean handkerchiefs have gone—the last person I need to hear from is the dog.

Play Dead: I'm admittedly squeamish about this accomplishment. I mean, suppose he became really *good* at it. You could go around for weeks remarking on how clever he is, only to take him in to get his rabies shot and have the vet tell you that it really isn't necessary, as he isn't playing after all.

 May 10

A whole new phenomenon is sweeping the nation. Mothers are going out to get a shampoo and set or buy a loaf of pumpernickel and simply disappearing for good.

I cannot imagine that every woman simply deserts the ship without leaving a note telling those left in command where the life jackets are stowed. A note, perhaps, like the following:

> Dear Jim:
> I promised to fix the children blueberry pancakes for breakfast. I'm not sure just where the spatula is; you might try looking in the toy box.
> Tommy has volunteered to bring cupcakes to Cubs tomorrow night. Bake forty-six chocolate and two white; chocolate gives Howie Sherman the hives.
> If the baby says "Wah-Wah" it means either "I want a drink of water" or "The dog is being sick again."
> Shirley owes us two onions. We owe Myra two

This Must Be the Weekend

extra-large disposable diapers, a vacuum cleaner bag, and a can of cream of mushroom soup.

It is Billy's turn to fill the ice cube trays and say grace. It is Karen's turn to drink out of the Fred Flintstone mug and plug in the vacuum cleaner.

The produce man will give you old lettuce for the guinea pig. Save any that isn't too brown for salads. The bird seed is in the liquor cabinet next to the fish food.

Thursday afternoon bridge is here next week. Barb bids a short club, and when Fran says "two no trump" it means she wishes she'd never opened in the first place. The sherry is in the liquor cabinet next to the bird seed.

Lots of luck,
Carol

 May 16

In addition to a poor sense of rhythm, abysmal coordination, and the inability to participate in "Row, Row, Row Your Boat" without putting my fingers in my ears, I lack a sense of timing.

I rush to get to the PTA meeting at 7:30 P.M. only to find that there is no one there but the janitor. I spend fifteen minutes helping him set up folding chairs.

The plumber promises to come early Monday morning. For the first time in recorded history, he arrives on time. Just after I have shampooed my hair and applied a Moondust Blonde rinse that must be washed out in ten minutes.

After thirty years of waiting in dentists' offices, thumbing through two-month-old news magazines and torn copies of *The Little Red Hen,* I arrive fifteen minutes late. Due to a last-minute cancellation, the dentist is right on schedule and charges me ten dollars for the time he has wasted.

For me, the distressing aspect of being invited to attend a dinner party is that one never is certain when to arrive.

What time, exactly, is "sixish"?

There is a distinct possibility of arriving at a "sixish" dinner party at 6:05, only to be greeted at the door by a four-year-old holding a TV dinner and a glass of Welch's Grape Juice, who tells you that Mommy is still fixing her face.

There is no need to ask where Daddy is. Daddy is the one in the tub yelling "Who the hell is that at the door?"

For the next forty-five minutes the three of you sit cross-legged on the living room floor, watching the last half of "The Bugs Bunny Roadrunner Hour," during which time you develop a nasty stiffness in your knees and an indelible spot of Welch's Grape Juice on your dress.

The next time you are invited to dinner at sixish, you resolve to play it safe and check first to see whether anyone else has arrived.

Seeing no parked cars in front of your host's house, you decide to drive around the block for a while. Unfortunately, the other guests do the same; by 10:00 P.M. there is a cavalcade of twelve cars glumly circling the block, each determined not to be the first to arrive.

The distraught hostess, meanwhile, has locked herself in the upstairs bathroom, where she is having a spectacular crying jag and making plans to move to another city, while her husband, having polished off two pitchers of before-dinner martinis, is finishing his eighth helping of lasagna.

Ideally one arrives at a party only after it is in full swing, when three people are sitting on the mantelpiece doing an imitation of a stop light, five others are pelting each other with smoked oysters, and a scholarly gentleman is trying to convince a young woman to let him pierce her ears. One can easily slip in virtually unnoticed and observe silently until one feels either stimulated enough to join in, or sufficiently bored to go home and watch *Godzilla vs. the Thing* on the late show.

Unfortunately, there are pitfalls in this situation as well, especially if your husband is wearing a sport coat and everyone else is in a suit.

'You didn't tell me to dress up!" he will hiss accusingly.

Now, I have precious little sympathy for a man who gets upset when his coat doesn't match his pants.

Especially when the other women are floating about in long gowns, while I am wearing stretch jeans, a turtleneck sweater, and Girl Scout socks.

But perhaps worst of all is our son's birthday party. Six children invariably arrive an hour early and are treated to a view of me blowing up balloons in my slip. They squat at my feet and exchange remarks on how neat the little red veins in my cheeks look.

 May 19

I decided, after beginning the garden last winter, that the first step toward a successful garden lies in conscientious soil preparation.

Every spring you will find that the typical garden yields the following crop of effluvia which evidently grew during the winter: one rusty skate key, six beef bones, a soggy Halloween mask, a Christmas card from Mimsy and Pudge, and half a jack-o'lantern.

Once you have harvested this bounty and put it into garbage bags, poke about in the dirt with a slotted spoon. Many purists will claim that one should use a rake or a spade instead. Disregard this nonsense. There are faddists in every discipline.

There is probably nothing more satisfying to the soul than turning over moist crumbles of black earth with a slotted spoon. Unfortunately, you do not have moist crumbles. You have solid clay, with a surface so impervious to manual disturbance that the slotted spoon rebounds from it with a force that

If It's Raining

loosens the fillings in your back teeth. Of course that occurs only when it is dry. After a rain, solid clay assumes the general consistency of Playdoh.

There is a remedy. One must add sufficient quantities of peat to loosen the soil. Peat is formed in bogs during a process that takes approximately two-million years. If you feel that you can't wait that long, however, you may buy it from a garden supply store.

While working in the peat, remind yourself that there is a lot to be said for growing your own vegatables. There is even more to be said against it, actually, but the human memory tends in a year to forget these disagreeable aspects. If it weren't for this fortunate mental lapse, not only would there be no tomatoes, but your brother would be an only child.

One of the more pleasant aspects of having a backyard garden is that it provides an acceptable topic of conversation should one encounter a neighbor out there.

"Certainly having a big problem with mealies on the conifers," my neighbor mused ruefully last week.

"Terrible! Worst I've ever seen!" I agreed, not having the vaguest idea whether a mealy is the weird red thing with six legs that I had just stepped on, or simply a dread fungus disease. It would have helped enormously if I could likewise identify a conifer, and possibly help them before the mealies got them all.

"Malathion," he declared, nodding his head solemnly. "Malathion's the answer."

"Perhaps," I countered guardedly, wondering what the question was and unwilling to give complete corroboration to something that might very well turn out to involve compulsory sterilization.

"It's got a great deal to do with acidity, you know," he confided. "Makes gardening a real chore."

"You can say that again," I agreed, musing that I can't even go to work without a glass of Alka-Seltzer, let alone garden.

"I've had a lot of luck putting compost on my privets," he announced, suddenly excited. "How about I come over and handle yours?"

"If my privets need handling, I'll do it myself," I stammered, backing away in terror.

"You don't use 2,4-D, do you?" he demanded.

"Certainly not!" I retorted haughtily as I stormed into the house. "I've never even tried marijuana!"

J *May 26*

Over the years, my daughter has formed an almost pathological attachment to the telephone.

While other toddlers romped through the playground clutching frayed security blankets, my daughter lumbered after them with a toy telephone wrapped around her neck.

When she was three, she slept with her left thumb in her mouth and her right forefinger in the telephone dial.

When she was in grade school, I allowed her to use the real telephone. Since not one of her friends was considered old enough to make or receive calls, she filled the gap by holding thirty-five-minute conversations with Dial-a-Prayer and a recorded time and weather message.

Now she has developed into a lovely young woman with sparkling blue eyes, golden blonde hair, and one ear which is noticeably flatter than the other.

More often than not, she and her friends don't even talk on the telephone. They play records. Or one holds the line while the other washes her hair. When they communicate verbally, the result is a series of cryptic one-liners:

"No!!!"

"He didn't!!!"

"My mother is even worse!!!"

Recently I had a telephone installed with an exceptionally long cord, which, like a trail of bread crumbs in the forest, I follow whenever I want her. It invariably leads to a closet.

If It's Raining

"Now hear this!" I bellow at the closed door. "I want my coat."

"I can't talk," a muffled voice replies. "*She's* listening."

 May 28

Everyone knows that mothers are indomitable characters who never get sick. After all, she is woman; she is invincible—except during the flu season.

There is something vaguely pathetic about an entire family expressing complete incredulity at her obvious vincibleness.

"Have you seen Mom?" one child said to the other. "She's been sitting there on the bathroom floor for a couple of hours."

"Doesn't she know it's time to peel the potatoes for dinner?"

"You don't imagine she's sick, do you?"

"Not her!" the other child hooted. I haughtily refuted his ill-considered diagnosis by passing out cold on the bathmat.

To my surprise, my loved ones assured me that I would be given every consideration while I was unwell.

Household chores were performed gratuitously. The family hockey player did the laundry between periods of a street hockey game. That's the day I discovered what a hockey puck sounds like at one hundred revolutions per minute.

To keep Mom warm and toasty, the hot water bottle was deposited on her chest, neatly removing whatever unsightly hair remained after the mustard plaster had done its job.

Medicine was dispensed promptly and ceremoniously. The doctor (the hockey player/laundress) entered the sickroom every day with "Time for your medicine, Madam. And how are we feeling today?"

Actually we had been feeling fine, until we discovered

that the doctor, capable as she was, had been regularly giving the dog my penicillin. I, on the other hand, had been fighting the flu with a daily ration of heart worm pills.

 May 31

One of the lessons a man learns very early in a relationship with a woman is how to avoid obnoxious household chores.

He can, of course, simply refuse to do anything the entire weekend except lie on the living room sofa with a bowl of pistachios on his chest and watch "Wide World of Sports" all day. He soon learns, however, that this attitude is likely to result in his spending all night on the sofa as well, and having to go to work on Monday morning with pistachio shell marks indelibly etched on his cheek.

The astute male, on the other hand, readily perceives the instrinsic value of "Botching." Botchers volunteer to fix absolutely everything, then proceed to break, wrap, wrench, or step through several key parts before throwing their backs out. It is somehow unthinkable to fault anyone with a positive attitude and a slipped disc.

The more sophisticated male will even manage to avoid grocery shopping. Asked to bring home a loaf of white bread, a bottle of catsup, and one pint of cottage cheese, he will arrive home with tuttie-frutti yogurt, frozen daiquiri mix, instant expresso coffee, and a gadget to cut melon balls. Not that he will forget what he went to buy. But instead of white bread and catsup, he will bring home Jewish rye and taco sauce. And instead of plain cottage cheese, he will buy cottage cheese with pineapple chunks. Which you won't notice until you've already used it in the lasagna.

If It's Raining

☂ *June 1*

I've been victimized by a vacuum cleaner. It entered my life as a $29.95 reconditioned Christmas present, which explains a good deal of my resentment. When one is expecting a pastel mink luxury and receives instead a used metal utility, it is something of a disappointment. In a mood of poisonous venom, I christened it Beaver, after a coat that I had hoped to give to the Salvation Army.

The first victim of Beaver's ministrations was a lightweight doormat which he attacked with vigor, inhaling not only string, thread, and dirt, but the entire rug itself. Beaver belched to a halt, the half-digested pink mat hanging out his hose. I finally induced him to give it up, resolving to confine his diet to meatier, less easily swallowed items like carpeting.

Beaver glided over the broadloom with ease, but it soon became apparent that he was picking and choosing. He flatly ignored Fuzzies like thread and dust balls, devoting himself to Hard Little Balls like crumbs and diamonds from engagement rings. I urged him on, murmuring encouraging noises when he balked at a Fuzzy. Still he refused, unless I first bent down and rolled the Fuzzy into a Hard Little Ball between my fingers. This method, while successful, was so time consuming and exhausting (rolling up dust balls manually is hard work) that I temporarily abandoned the carpet in favor of the hardwood.

After carefully hiding my bedroom throw rugs, remem-

This Must Be the Weekend   75

bering Beaver's penchant for the doormat, I changed his attachment to the one to be used for floors. Oh, yes, Beaver came with all manner of goodies. He has, besides the floor and rug attachments, a drapery brush, paint sprayer, and a tiny brush for removing belly-button lint.

Beaver was noisy doing the carpets; on hardwood floors he wailed like a banshee. After answering a call from the SPCA and assuring them that I wasn't declawing my cat with pliers, I resumed the task. He did reasonably well, to a point. Or more exactly, to a corner. His attachment, while doing a great job on the straight-away, wouldn't touch into the corners. Consequently over the years, all manner of corruption has accumulated there. After all, I'm pretty well tied up rolling dust balls for Beaver, and I can't do everything by hand.

 June 4

I don't believe that when I was little any adult ever worried about communicating with me. Present-day child psychologists warn against this and plead with parents to become pals with their children while still retaining parental authority. This is about as easy as whistling "Bye-Bye Blackbird" with a mouth full of Tokay grapes.

I tried communicating with our daughter, Laurie, but I couldn't get past threesies at jacks, and when I stood on my head I got a nosebleed. Not only was I a pretty hopeless pal, but I found that it's hard to retain parental authority while you're hemorrhaging on your last clean blouse. When I nearly strangled myself trying to skip Double Dutch, Laurie got a pained expression on her face and asked whether she could be excused to go and do her homework.

I decided that my husband would have more success with our son Eric.

"What do you mean, I don't communicate with him?" my husband exclaimed. "I said 'hello' to him just yesterday."

"I mean really communicate. Sit down and talk to him. Find out what he thinks."

"I know what he thinks. He thinks his sister is a creep. He said so at supper. He also thinks that Brussels sprouts taste like paint remover."

"Don't you ever share your opinions with him?" I asked.

"I shared my opinion that he'd better eat his Brussels sprouts even if they do taste like paint remover."

"That's not what I mean. You should share your views on life and establish a meaningful relationship."

"All right," he sighed, "I'll try." Half an hour later he returned, holding a bloody handkerchief to his nose.

"It was going pretty well. He showed me his bubblegum wrappers, and I let him look at my *Playboy* centerfold collection. Then he asked me whether I could stand on my head. I think we could have established a meaningful relationship if my nose just hadn't started bleeding."

 June 12

As one of the joys of summer lies in acquiring a golden-brown complexion, the following is a layman's guide to sun-tanning:

Where to Tan: The question of where to do your tanning depends largely on how you look partially clothed. Consult a full-length mirror, inquiring "Mirror, mirror, made of glass, am I too fat across the shoulders?"

If the mirror replies "Speaking objectively, you look exactly like a giant, albino elephant," it may be wise to conduct your sun-worshipping from a strictly private area, perhaps the inside of the packing case from a grand piano.

What to Wear: Most people choose a small bathing suit While it is permissible to lie on your stomach and undo the bra hooks to avoid the offending white stripe, bear in mind that you cannot jump up quickly when an enormous, hairy spider crawls across the back of your thigh.

What to Do while Tanning: Since you invariably feel silly lying there simmering in the sun like a gigantic rump roast, it is necessary to find something to take your mind off how ridiculous you feel and how unbearably hot you are.

You may try reading a book. If it is sunny enough to tan, however, it is too sunny to read, as the letters tend to cavort about the page like hyperactive fireflies and form idiotic sentences like "Srum, whep heliop das freezen."

You could invite someone to tan with you, preferably someone whiter, ideally someone inclined toward blotches or freckles. Never invite anyone with an olive complexion who will turn golden brown in thirty-five minutes while you lie there encased in skin that is the same attractive hue as the underbelly of a mackerel.

You could always drink. But since one drink in the sun is equivalent to two in the shade, there is a distinct possibility that after one Planter's Punch you will not be able to get out of the chaise longue, and will have to lie there all afternoon, helplessly chortling over the sentence, "Srum, whep helip das freezen."

June 13

I am becoming more and more convinced that the entire new wave of women's journalism is dedicated to making me feel inferior.

A few years ago, women's magazines only left me feeling slightly uneasy over my unimaginative meals, my inability to

If It's Raining

knit drapes, and my ignorance of how to remove the ten most common household stains. I realized my shortcomings, but I could cope. "Wood nymphs," I used to declare loftily, "don't embroider pillowcases."

But recently even the most staid women's magazines have begun to insist upon zeroing in on my love life.

One recent article spent several thousand libido-provoking words informing me that stopping smoking would vastly whet my sexual appetite. While I was almost ready to quit before reading the article, now I'm positively embarrassed to give up smoking. I mean, suppose someone offered me a cigarette. As soon as I said that I'd given them up, everyone would say "Ah hah!" and start snickering and nudging each other.

Worst of all, these magazines are showing me new, vital areas in which I am woefully unimaginative and ignorant.

It's all very well to declare oneself completely disinterested in the problems of interfacing a knit suit, but can anyone safely ignore an article entitled "Twelve Common Sexual Hang-Ups and How to Cure Them"?

Then again, suppose I *do* read the article.

While I can live with the knowledge that I am incapable of growing African Violets, can I likewise handle the realization that, out of twelve common sexual hang-ups, I have ten? All incurable?

 June 14

Recently I ran across an article giving complete instructions on how to apply natural makeup.

Armed with twenty-eight dollars worth of nonmakeup, I resolved to try.

The article stated that I must first contour my face. "A judicious application of blusher," the article maintained, "can effectively create the illusion of slimness." Reasoning that a judicious application of blusher certainly sounded far simpler than losing ten pounds, I began contouring. Unfortunately, the resulting illusion did not make me look slimmer, only in desperate need of a shave.

I likewise tried to raise my cheekbones by "artfully applying a darker foundation in the hollows below them." After fifteen minutes of intense searching, during which I discovered that I *have* no hollows, I chose random spots where I reasoned hollows should be. I only succeeded in looking dirty.

"Gleamer," the article asserted, "will impart the aura of dewy youth when carefully applied to the upper corners of the cheeks." Not only did gleamer look suspiciously like a grease stick, but it struck me as being nothing but a tube full of the very thing that I had just applied powder to cover up. The resulting impression was not so much that I possessed dewy youth, more that I had just played five straight sets of tennis.

"Eyes," the article warned, "need special attention. The darkest shade is brushed on next to the upper lashes, the lighter above it, the lightest stretching to the brow to raise and accentuate it." I soon discovered that while it is impossible to apply eye shadow to an open eye, it is likewise impossible to apply eye shadow with both eyes closed. One must apply it to a closed eye, while the other one watches to make sure you are doing it right.

While I rather like the overall effect, I have found that it takes me a good forty-five minutes of frantic activity to achieve the appearance that I am wearing nothing but radiant good health.

 June 15

Many women these days tend to belittle the positive side of homemaking, overlooking the very real benefits of a homemaker's complete autonomy.

If It's Raining

Aside from being the supreme arbiter of whether the toilet paper should unroll from underneath or over the top, a woman is free to determine when the vacuum cleaner bag is full and which socks do, indeed, match.

But perhaps the most heady aspect of being home alone all day is that you are able to engage in all manner of whimsies, up to and including petty vices, without the risk that someone will come roaring around the corner and warn you that what you are doing is tasteless, stupid, and will more than likely give you acne, or worse.

For instance, if I go back to bed every morning at nine o'clock, no one will know, unless I don't get up in time for the chenille marks to vanish before the children come home for lunch.

I can watch soap operas. I mean, there is no possibility of appreciating the tragic nuances of "As the World Turns" when a ten-year-old is sitting on the sofa going "yuk!!"

I can do exercises. One simply cannot do a successful bend and stretch when a preschooler is chortling "Make your tummy jiggle again, Mommy!"

I can go into the bathroom without closing the door.

And I can wear anything I choose. Or nothing at all, which my next-door neighbor swears not only cuts down beautifully on her weekly laundry, but adds a certain titillation to even such mundane chores as matching up socks.

 June 17

People constantly express admiration for a small child who appears to be socially at ease in the presence of a large number of adults.

Nonsense.

A child in the company of adults is faced with a group of well-wishers who are genuinely concerned with making him feel that his presence is a welcome addition. Any child exhibiting the most rudimentary social graces is treated to a degree of praise which an adult achieves only by climbing the north side of a mountain or inscribing the entire New Testament on a ping-pong ball in Chinese.

"Imagine that!" they will exclaim. "I asked him his age, and he said 'six.' What a kid!"

Personally, I reserve my admiration for any adult who can stay in a room full of six-year-olds for ten minutes without bursting into tears, breaking out in a rash, or retreating to the bathroom and locking the door for the next two hours.

An adult in the company of small children is faced with a group of potential terrorists who vacillate between ignoring his presence completely and regarding him as an enemy spy.

Any questions directed toward the adult will be on the order of "Where did you get those funny wrinkles in your neck?"

 June 19

I hate to see my children watch too much TV.

It's not the sex and violence I mind. For a child who has been raised on blind mice having their tails lopped off with butcher knives, "Kojak" is pretty tame stuff.

No, what I find to be thoroughly objectionable and potentially disillusioning are commercials.

Parents in commercials are unfailingly loyal. Who but someone in a commercial would refuse to take twice as much of another laundry soap rather than switch from Tide? I mean, twice as much is twice as much; so what if the white socks are gray for the next two months?

Parents in commercials are unfailingly cheerful. When you climb into a tar pit ten minutes before you are to leave for Grandma's house, a TV mother will merely chuck you under the chin and call you a "Bold One," rather than going all white around the mouth and locking herself in the bathroom.

If It's Raining

Parents in commercials are always patient. When you, sixteen of your friends, and an enormous English sheep dog barge into the kitchen and drip muddy water onto a freshly waxed floor, a TV mother fixes everyone a huge pitcher of Kool-Aid instead of sobbing "Get out of the kitchen this minute, and take that lousy mutt with you!"

Finally, mothers in commercials are pretty. Since I am secretly sure that all TV children are really thirty-five-year-old midgets anyway, it is probably logical that their mothers all look twenty-two. But no mother that I know ever greeted her children at breakfast wearing blue eyeshadow. Not unless she had been to a party the night before and had been too tired to wash her face.

June 20

Personally, I am opposed to using grass.

Now I know perfectly well that thousands of respectable, taxpaying citizens not only delight in grass, but experience no physical or mental problems connected with it.

But for myself, I favor doing the entire backyard over in green cement.

I resent grass. I resent administering constant protection, dedicated feeding, and conscientious watering to anything that neither calls me "Mommy" nor licks my hand in gratitude.

Every spring, the backyard emerges from the snow, thickly matted with a lichenlike underbelly of winter's casualties, which must be meticulously combed from the lawn while it is still cold enough outside to make your nose run.

Any greenish bits that haven't become wedged in the rake and uprooted must be slavishly pandered to immediately, plied with organic fertilizer, and encouraged to spread sufficiently to fill in the inevitable bald spots.

Actually, after sufficient ministrations, the bald spots fill in remarkably rapidly—with chickweed. One is sorely tempted to simply give over to the chickweed, it being obviously fitter, as well as a great deal prettier, than grass. This will never do. Darwin aside, one can't go around liking chickweed, even pretty chickweed.

Once an exquisite green carpet is established, it must be watched like an eccentric uncle, lest it suddenly exhibit dangerous aberrations, and must never be left unattended for extended period of time.

And for what? All six patio chairs have to be put on an eight-by-ten slab of cement, because every time you sit on the exquisite green carpet, ants crawl up your legs.

One of the saddest misconceptions about gardening is that, while shrubs and trees are constantly demanding mulch and clamoring to have their terminal buds scratched, grass is simply laid down like wall-to-wall broadloom and forgotten.

It would help, of course, if once a lawn was laid out flat, it would remain flat instead of sinking in some places, heaving in others, and generally carrying on like a harpooned whale. Concealed hollows invariably contain potential hazards; more than one mower has been summarily abandoned with the dog's beef bone or leash jammed irrevocably between its blades. To make matters worse, someone in the family always insists on installing lily ponds at the bottoms of inclines, ponds just deep enough to engulf a fast-running mower up to the handles.

One of the first problems of lawn care is whether to leave the clippings on the lawn or remove them. Half your neighbors will maintain that the clippings provide the lawn with nutrients; the other half will insist that accumulated clippings deprive the lawn of necessary sunshine. Whatever your inclinations, do not argue with anyone wielding pruning shears.

If you do choose to remove the clippings, you will need a grass catcher, which is a piece of striped awning material hooked onto the mower. When it is not falling off, the catcher collapses periodically and must be kicked along with your free foot. This flattens the grass nicely so that the mower rolls harmlessly over, accomplishing nothing but raising a blister on your thumb.

Actually the disposition of clippings is rarely a problem as, more often than not, the green grass doesn't grow all around. Instead of forming a verdant carpet under the elm tree, it concentrates exclusively on poking itself up through the cracks in the front walk, and your entire lawn maintenance program will consist of digging it out with a fish fork.

 June 22

When my parents noticed my marked tendency to bump into our door frames and wave to people's backs, they thought that I was simply stupid and clumsy.

Later, when I started school, they discovered that, in addition to being stupid and clumsy, I needed glasses.

After ten years of wearing glasses with lenses approximately as thick as the bottoms of coke bottles, I was fitted with a pair of contact lenses. I don't have to wear my contact lenses all the time. Only when I want to see.

Last Saturday afternoon, I was in the supermarket, leaning over the meat counter and wondering what tripe was and whether we were desperate enough to eat it, when my left contact lens fell into a pile of frozen pork chops.

"Hold on there!" I exclaimed grabbing a package of chops from an elderly lady. "My eye is on these."

"Not bloody likely, Toots!" she snapped, snatching them back, "I saw 'em first!"

While my attention was diverted during this caustic exchange, there must have been a veritable run on pork chops.

"Oh, no!" I shrieked, patting the now-empty compartment.

"Don't take it so hard, lady," the butcher said, patting my hand consolingly. "Why don't you try some nice spare ribs instead?"

"You don't understand! My left contact lens fell in there," I bawled, pointing to the meat counter.

"No fooling!" he replied, peering into the counter. "That's

tough. Tell you what, though," he added brightly, "I'll give you a rain check on the pork chops."

Shortly after that, I arrived for my long-awaited appointment with an optometrist.

"Doctor will see you right away," his nurse announced.

Resisting the urge to genuflect, I fumbled my way into the examination room, banging my shoulder painfully on the door frame.

After first noting the vital information—whether I preferred to pay cash or charge it, Doctor instructed me to look at his right ear while he peered into my eye from a distance of three inches with a tiny flashlight.

"Your eye seems perfectly normal," he announced.

"So does your ear," I replied politely. He placed my chin in an enormous black machine.

"I want you to read the chart for me. What line can you read?"

"The one that says 'Made in Germany.' "

"Where do you see that?"

"Here," I pointed to a sign on the machine one inch above my nose.

"Look at the chart," he said, pointing to a fuzzy square of light at the far end of the room. "Tell me which is better, this," he said, changing lenses, "or this?"

One half-hour and twenty-seven agonizing decisions later, he announced that while I couldn't pick up the lens for a week, he would loan me something to use in the meantime.

While I'm quite eager to get my new lens, I don't expect to get a seat on the bus nearly so often once I give back the white cane he lent me.

June 25

I am desperately searching for the perfect summer camp —for myself.

If It's Raining

I have come to the realization that I would much rather learn three dozen secret Indian hand signals than ten ways to remove tar spots from T-shirts.

I would like to spend my summer identifying birds, not skin rashes.

And I would much rather be lulled to sleep by a chorus of crickets than by the intemperate revelry at a pool party to which I wasn't invited.

I have never understood why summer camps are restricted to children, while their mothers are the ones who have been confined for the preceding ten months and suffer from tired blood and hot flashes. Like youth itself, summer camp is wasted on the young. The last time my son went to summer camp, it cost me $250 to have someone teach him to short-sheet a bed.

Ideally, campers should all be mothers, with first priority given to women who are over thirty-five and at least three inches too short for their weight. We seasoned mothers would make excellent campers. The challenge of making a campfire out of two sticks would be simple for anyone who, whenever the tweezers are missing, can pick gravel out of somebody's knee with a pair of ice tongs.

Not only would we not have to bring rubber sheets, but no mother in her right mind would ever complain about any food that someone else had cooked, even if it does have saltpeter in it.

 *June 26*

"We don't need lunches today, Mom," my son informed me gently at seven o'clock this morning.

"Of course you need lunches. You can't expect to learn how to take the square root of pi on an empty stomach," I retorted, deftly turning the heels of the bread to the inside and hoping he wouldn't notice.

"But school's out," he protested.

"Out!?!?" I gasped.

"For the summer."

"For the entire summer!?!?" I bleated, clutching a kosher dill pickle to my breast.

"Yeah. Isn't that super? Do you know what I'm going to do?"

"Judging by past experience, you'll step on a rusty nail, sit on your glasses, and pitch a baseball through the window of the Presbyterian rectory. And tomorrow will be even more eventful."

"You don't sound glad that we're out," he sniffed.

"Glad? Why shouldn't I be glad? After all, when you're in school I never get to visit with the staff at the emergency ward or the optometrist's office, let alone have a heart-to-heart talk with the Presbyterian minister about the Decaying Moral Values of Today's Youth."

"This summer is going to be different," he promised loftily. "You forget how I've matured during this past year."

While his statement would have been a great deal more effective had he not jumped off the garage roof two hours later, he was right about one thing. With two broken arms, this summer is certainly going to be different.

 June 27

A is for aphids, the greenish things floating in the pitcher of lemonade.

B is for bulbs, those nasty, onionish globs you found in the basement when you moved into the house. At the first sign of spring, unearth them, and throw them in the garbage.

C is for cuttings, those lovely green sprigs of other people's plants which you snip off carefully, wrap neatly in wet newspaper, and proceed to leave on the car dashboard in the

If It's Raining

sun for two weeks.

D is for dandelions. Dandelions must be recognized for the noxious weeds they are. Right-thinking people do not like dandelions, even though they are obviously hardier, and a great deal prettier, than zinnias.

E is for evergreen. Evergreen trees do not have leaves that turn majestic shades of gold and red every autumn, then fall to earth and form a gentle carpet of color. Hooray for evergreen trees.

F is for fences, the longish lengths of splintery wood and/or rusty wire over which one throws largish stones and the soggy tennis balls the dog has sucked on.

G is for geraniums, which are either the blackish sticks poking out of the ground beside the weeping birch or the moldy pot of "stuff" in the basement, depending on whether anyone remembered to lift and pot them last fall. Throw them into the garbage beside the bulbs.

H is for hoses, the long ropes of hollow plastic caught in the lawn mower.

I is for ivy, luxuriant, glossy vines which adhere to brick walls, create an aura of verdant beauty, and pull the mortar out.

J is for July, the month in which it is too hot to do all those things that it was too cold to do in January.

K is for kompost, a word which, as this is my book, I can spell any way I choose. Kompost is what nongardeners refer to as garbage.

L is for lawn mower, which, although it wouldn't cut hot butter, has somehow managed during the winter to nibble through the plastic hose in thirty-six places. The term may also be applied to a male child under eighteen, should you be fortunate enough to have one.

M is for manure, which is called organic fertilizer because it sounds nicer.

N is for nemophila, which, although it sounds uncomfortably like something Nice People don't do, is actually a flower. Trust me.

O is for organic fertilizer (*see manure*).

P is for parties which gardeners can now have outside. Outdoor parties are nice in that you don't have to vacuum afterwards.

R is for run over, which is what you probably have done to the threaded metal end of the hose, irrevocably preventing it from screwing into the water outlet.

S is for sprinklers, capriciously shaped metal and/or plastic objects which either refuse to sweep from side to side or refuse to spin. Either is equally effective at delivering water in such an erratic manner that the flowering crab will become shriveled and desiccated while the petunias will wash away into the gutter. Or they would if you hadn't run over the metal end of the hose.

T is for toolshed, an unassembled metal contraption which, when erected, will be only half the size of the shed in the illustration. Toolsheds come with instruction sheets. Three pages of instructions, all labeled "Page 2" and beginning "Now that you have the walls erected . . . "

U is for urea formaldehyde, a type of plant food, the generous application of which is guaranteed to keep Avon from calling.

V is for verbena, which sounds a lot prettier than it looks.

W is for weed killer, an appallingly expensive chemical which must never be applied unless it is pouring rain and perfectly still, so that it can't blow onto the roses or a loved one.

X is for the bare spot in the lawn where the builders buried their beer cans.

Y is for yellow. Carrots should be; broccoli shouldn't.

Z is for your zone, which you soon discover that everything you just planted isn't hardy for.

J *June 30*

I have given up smoking.

Actually, I was fairly certain that I had given up smoking

six weeks ago. Being fairly certain you've given up smoking is like being fairly certain you're pregnant; it doesn't do to go around broadcasting the fact until you're absolutely certain.

There is nothing so unnerving to someone who suspects she may be either pregnant or giving up smoking than to have half a dozen concerned friends and relatives bleating, "Yeah, but are you *sure*?" every fifteen minutes.

I realized, too, that should I discover that the decision was a Dreadful Mistake, I could simply change my mind a week or so down the line without having to listen to anyone sigh and shake his head.

Besides, anyone who has given up cigarettes is twitchy enough for the first few days without having several people watching him covertly from behind copies of *Time* magazine, hoping to catch him in the throes of some sort of disgusting withdrawal symptom.

These same people peremptorily decide, in your best interests, either to hide your last pack of cigarettes, or to flush them dramatically down the toilet.

It does very little good to explain to these people that you *need* a last pack of cigarettes lying around waiting not to be smoked, that will power is not born of deprivation, and that as soon as they leave, you intend to tear the lining out of the pockets of every coat in the house to glean enough tobacco to make one final cigarette not to smoke.

July 2

    I only say "no" to our children when I'm absolutely forced to, when my back is against the wall, and they're clamoring to dye their eyebrows black, or have "Make Love Not War" tattooed on their forearms.

    But I'm far from being an overpermissive pushover. I don't say "yes," either.

    Instead, I've become a master at using the parental equivocation of "we'll see," which has the convenient ambiguity of meaning anything from "probably" to "fat chance."

    I have found that only immediate problems demand an immediate response, and if necessary I can be quite forceful. As proof, I offer the following actual conversation:

    "Can I have a chocolate chip cookie?"

    "How do you ask?"

    "*May* I have a chocolate chip cookie?"

    "What do you say?"

    "May I *please* have a chocolate chip cookie?"

    "No. It's too close to supper."

    The situations which are bona fide "we'll sees" are requests involving future events. I find it virtually impossible to project beyond what I'm going to fix for supper; anything after that is clearly in the lap of the gods.

    Last week the children approached me as I was de-lumping horseradish sauce by forcing it through the tea strainer.

(Note to children: Never ask Mommy *anything* while she is straining horseradish sauce. Mommy is always nervous and out of sorts at moments like this.)

"Let's go see *King Kong Meets the Creature from the Black Lagoon* and a *Daffy Duck* cartoon carnival at the drive-in on Saturday." Now at that moment I would rather have been hung by my heels over a live volcano than sit through *King Kong Meets the Creature from the Black Lagoon*, to say nothing about the *Daffy Duck* cartoon carnival. But after all, it was only Tuesday. Long before Saturday they might forget about it or the drive-in might be razed for a shopping mall.

"We'll see," I said. I wasn't really too worried. If they asked again on Saturday I could always employ the best answer of all: "Ask your Daddy."

 July 7

Judging by the sales fliers we receive daily, everyone worth knowing is assembling his own metal toolshed.

Before ordering a box of shed, remember that when erected it will be only half the size of the shed in the illustration, as those two adults standing beside the shed in the picture are actually twenty-five inch high midgets named Sam and Zelda. Sam and Zelda earn $37,000 a year being photographed while sitting in above-ground swimming pools and illustrating adequate head room in camper-trailers.

This discrepancy is not immediately obvious, however, as the contents seem adequate to construct a medium-sized elementary school, there being at least three roofs, ten windows, and 637 assorted wing nuts, bolts, and screws, half of which spill out of the box and roll under the front porch.

You will notice right off that since the screw holes don't match, you must drill 243 new holes, thus giving the shed the

This Must Be the Weekend

same jaunty air as if it had been strafed by a machine gun.

Anyone with the normal complement of arms will need help erecting the walls, as all four have to be joined at once, a feat roughly equivalent to making a house of playing cards in a windstorm. While it is possible to use a friend's arms, remember that after you snarl "I said to hold it straight, you incompetent nincompoop!" three or four times, he won't be your friend anymore. Good friends are hard to find. Better use your wife's arms.

As you go along, you can even imply that it is her fault that all the original glass has shrunk down to a window the size of a shaving mirror and that the door meets only at the top. Actually you will find that it is such a serviceable shed that you may even sleep in it for the next three nights. It's ever so much nicer than the doghouse.

 July 13

The unfortunate fact of the matter is that an actual camping trip rarely resembles those photographs of rustic togetherness which features Dad, Mom, and a brace of children sitting around a camp fire toasting wienies as the setting sun turns the sky into a symphony of color.

Of course, no one would ever go camping if they showed someone beside a fire taking a sitz bath in a two-quart saucepan. Or a candid shot of a garter snake crawling up Mom's pant leg while she is busy picking gnats out of the butter.

Anyway, you can't light a fire when it's pouring rain. On the one day it doesn't rain, the children, having announced that they have already seen a sunset once, insist on eating in the tent and reading comic books.

Now a tent is just like a bedroom. A tiny little bedroom. One that leaks. You share this tiny little leaky bedroom with three other people, one who twitches, one who snores, and a five-year-old who had six cans of pop before retiring. Not to mention four pairs of wet tennis shoes and a dog who has spent the better part of the day rolling in dead fish.

Next to a giant economy-size can of Raid, a camper's most valuable asset is a short memory. By the time he has silently folded up his tent and eased his scratched, mosquito-bitten body gingerly into the car to go home, he will have completely forgotten the agony of stubbing his big toe on a tent stake at 3:00 A.M., while taking a five-year-old to the comfort station, and will begin babbling rapturously about how lovely the pine trees looked in the moonlight.

 July 14

To my way of thinking, swimming is less of a sport than something I do when I fall out of a boat.

It is most uncomfortable to find myself standing in water that is ten-feet deep, when I am only five-and-a-half-feet deep. In such a situation, swimming is infinitely more practical than walking, as walking requires the rather tedious process of continuously sinking to the bottom and hopping up high enough for my nose to clear the surface.

Floating—a process which involves lying back and filling my lungs with air—I have found to be a most unsatisfactory alternative, for while my lungs float beautifully, from the neck up and the hips down I am completely submerged. And not having mastered the art of breathing through my navel, I panic.

Actually, I restrict my aquatic activities to a rudimentary crawl and an admittedly abortive backstroke.

In order to do the crawl, you must scoop handfuls of water backward and duck your head periodically under your armpit to breathe, all the while executing a leg-motion rather like you would use to shake free of a gigantic man-eating squid.

Personally, I prefer the backstroke.

The major drawback to the backstroke is that lying on your back cuts down drastically on your field of vision, it being restricted to viewing cloud formations and a stray bird or two. The one time I was foolish enough to immerse my body in a swimming pool, I found myself suddenly in the deep end. Worse yet, I was in the middle of an impromptu game of water polo. I believe that I lost my taste for swimming immediately after the ball landed on my chest and fifteen people yelled "Mine!"

 July 24

It is fatal to confess to anyone that you are thinking of going on a diet.

"You're nuts," one of my equally overweight friends declared as she handed me a second helping of devil's food cake. "It's taken you years of haggling to acquire a decent wardrobe tailored to your build. What are you going to do with a closet full of pantsuits with size eight jackets and size sixteen pants?"

"You don't look *that* bad," declared one of my very slim friends. (Narrow people are prone to sadism.) "What's your waist?"

"You mean *where's* my waist?" I replied morosely. "I haven't got one."

"Don't be silly. Everyone has a waist. It's about six inches below your bust."

"I don't have one of those, either," I wailed.

Only my children offered anything remotely approaching moral support.

"That's a terrific idea," my son agreed, spearing my second pork chop neatly off my plate.

"Great news!" echoed my daughter. "Can I have your dessert?"

While gluttony, like lust, is one of the Seven Deadly Sins, it is not nearly so easily assuaged by three dozen push-ups and a cold shower.

Initially, I attempted to sublimate my unnatural cravings by turning to television, only to have my favorite programs interrupted every ten minutes by Kraft food commercials featuring someone folding three cups of mayonnaise into a bowl full of melted caramels and miniature marshmallows.

The success of any diet is utterly dependent on the degree of your ability to convince your stomach that it is, in fact, full, so that it does not take umbrage and seize up on you.

Stomachs, fortunately, are the most stupid organ of the entire human body, forced to rely very heavily on messages received from your nose and mouth.

The following are three extremely simple mealtime strategies designed to confuse the stomach:

1. Chew each bite 3,427 times. Eaten this way, one-half a cup of cottage cheese will so exhaust your jaw that it will immediately jump to the conclusion that it has consumed a seven-course dinner.

2. If you feel you must use the good china for dinner, do not serve yourself on a standard-size dinner plate, as the sight of all those hand-painted flowers peeking through the peas will only emphasize the spartan size of your portions. Much more visual deception results from eating your entire dinner from the lid of a jar of Cheese Whiz.

3. Ten minutes before your evening meal, lick the glue off a whole box of airmail envelopes.

 July 26

It seems that an inordinate amount of media coverage has been devoted to the problems of gays.

Personally, I have nothing against gays.

I mean, I certainly wouldn't want someone waking me up every morning by whistling "Happy Days Are Here Again" in my left ear, but a little gaiety in moderation is hardly cause for such violent emotions as are being displayed these days.

Gays, fortunately, are attracted to each other. Anyone who can tumble down a flight of steps, break his ankle in three places, and knock out four teeth, yet express delight that his Timex is still running, would find himself to be completely incompatible with a person who goes all white around the mouth if there's dew on his morning paper.

I think, while everyone agrees that two consenting adults should be free to be as gay as they please, no one should be forced to spend time with a person who tap-dances while he brushes his teeth.

Anita Bryant contends that should we allow gays to educate our children, they, too could become gay. I must admit that the thought does give one pause. The average mother has enough to do without having to contend with a brace of ten-year-olds calling her "Marmee" and being gay all over the back of her neck while she is down on her hands and knees, wiping grape jelly off the kitchen floor.

Which reminds me, while I've known several gay men, I have met very few women who were anything more than affable. Maybe it has something to do with having to spend a whole lifetime matching socks.

July 27

One of the major concerns facing our society is the growing rate of marriage breakdowns.

While lack of communication is frequently cited as the underlying cause in many cases, I am certain that there is a more basic problem.

Too many Night People marry Morning People.

Such marriages are effectively doomed from the start.

Your basic morning person arrives home at 5:30 P.M. Tripping over the bags under his eyes, he stumbles through the front door in a somnambulistic trance, only to be greeted by a Night Person humming "Come to the Cabaret" while clenching a flower between her teeth.

While Morning People retire at 9:30 P.M., Night People stay up until 2:30 A.M. to watch *The Man in the Iron Mask* for the fifth time.

When the alarm clock rings at 6:30 A.M., the Morning Person will vault gaily from bed just in time to witness the Night Person fling the clock to the floor and stomp on it until his feet bleed.

Morning People eat things like omelettes and waffles for breakfast. Night People begin the day with two Excedrin tablets dissolved in a glass of Carnation Instant.

While their friends respect Morning People, they rarely call them long distance at 3:00 A.M. to wish them a Happy Saint Swithin's Day.

It is just as difficult for a Night Person to establish rapport with a person who views his body as a temple as it is for a Morning Person to communicate meaningfully with someone who has no discernible stomach muscles.

 July 28

For many women, holding down a full-time job has become an economic necessity.

Aside from the many mothers these days who have chosen careers outside their homes as a means of personal fulfillment, at least an equal number enter the work force simply to make ends meet.

But no matter what motivation causes a woman to combine motherhood with a full-time career, one common, inherent difficulty is the gnawing guilt one feels at mealtime.

"This is a TV dinner!" my son announced last night, pointing accusingly at his plate.

"What makes you think that?" I demanded, doggedly maintaining an air of righteous indignation, even though I knew full well that there were three still-warm divided foil trays hidden in the bottom of the garbage can. "How can you tell?"

"I don't have to chew the gravy."

"I feel so bad about this," I remarked later, slicing off three pieces of Sara Lee chocolate cake. "With me working full time, you never get homemade biscuits any more. You never sit down to spaghetti sauce that's simmered all afternoon, or help me roll out the dough for a homemade apple pie."

"I wouldn't feel so bad about it, Mom," my daughter retorted, patting my hand consolingly. "You never fixed any of those things before you started working full time, either."

 July 30

Perhaps it's my own lack of savoir faire, but I always seem to have an inordinate amount of trouble in restaurants.

The maitre d' invariably leads me to a table behind a pillar, in a draft, or right next to the men's room, a table at which no one else will sit. If he were to ask whether this table suited madame, possibly madame might timidly venture the opinion that, although she doesn't want to be a bother, she'd prefer another one. One with four legs, perhaps, rather than three.

Of course, he doesn't ask. Rather he fixes me with a gaze

so steely that it is obvious that, should I dare to complain, he will report me directly to the manager.

Once I am seated, my problems are not over. After twenty minutes, the waiter casually saunters over, picking his teeth with his forefinger, to take my order.

"I'll have the lamb chops," I venture. The waiter shakes his head.

"The chops are bad today. I suggest the stuffed tripe." Without waiting for a reply, he leaves. Now if there's anything I loathe, it's tripe, even stuffed tripe. Somehow I lack the panache to fling a bread stick at his retreating form and demand lamb chops.

One hour later my stuffed tripe appears. It has evidently tumbled off en route and been scraped up off the floor, as it is covered with light green carpet fluff. The waiter glares at me as if I am somehow personally responsible for staining his carpet. He slips the bill under my plate obviously hinting that the sooner a troublemaker like me leaves, the better.

☂ *August 1*

Many of you undoubtedly just suffered through the harrowing experience of moving.

Before you begin congratulating yourself on having survived it all, make certain that you have ordered telephone installation. If not, you are facing probably the greatest trauma of the entire move.

"We have just moved to 3131 Hartwell Crescent, and I would like to order a telephone," you say, inwardly praising yourself on your forthright approach.

Unfortunately the disembodied voice of the business office shatters your aplomb by crooning, "How many rooms do you have in your new home?"

She might as well have asked how many second cousins your great-grandmother had. "Seven?" you quaver, it sounding like a likely number. "Nine or ten if you count bathrooms and kitchens."

"How many bedrooms do you have?" she purrs.

What ever is she driving at, you wonder, your cheeks reddening as you blurt out "four."

"My, that sounds lovely," she coos.

"It is rather nice," you admit modestly. "There's a wet bar in the basement, which is an authentic replica of an Old English . . . "

"You'll need at least six telephones," she announces.

If It's Raining

"Hmmmm?" Your reverie shatters abruptly.

"That's one for each bedroom, one for the kitchen, and one for the Old Eng . . . "

"One phone," you insist.

"*One* phone!?" she gasps incredulously. "But you can't possibly . . . "

"One phone!" you insist.

"Would you like a touch-tone, Contempra, or our enchanting Princess-style with a lighted dial? Each comes in your choice of seven decorator colors—Seamist Green, Beautiful Beige, Sunrise Yellow, Pristine White, Achingly Aqua, Bucolic Blue, or Scarlett O'Hara."

"I'd like a plain black one. It should ring."

"Black?" she shudders audibly.

"Black is my favorite color."

"I'm sorry, but it will take six weeks to special order a plain black phone. We just delivered the only one in stock to a mortuary."

☂ *August 3*

Every family must of necessity adopt some sort of position regarding weekend meals. One popular attitude is the laissez faire approach, whereby everyone over six years of age eats whatever he likes whenever he finds himself passing the refrigerator.

Unfortunately, left to their own dietary whimsies, people tend to ignore refrigerator jars full of leftover chicken a la king in favor of wolfing down huge slabs of the roast beef that you had hoped to stretch out through next Wednesday.

And there is always one member of every family who will shun anything vaguely nutritional and exist the entire weekend on a diet of marshmallows.

But those families who insist upon having three formal, sit-down type meals a day find themselves lacking a quorum more often than not.

People tend to rise on weekends as the spirit calls them. Our son's spirit calls at 7:00 A.M., while our daughter's spirit is completely mum until 11:00 A.M. An unwary mother may find herself faced with a steady rivulet of people trickling in asking for waffles with blueberry syrup all morning. By 11:30 the waffle iron is overheated, and mother isn't far behind.

Lunchtime is even worse. Everyone takes to whizzing through the kitchen on their way to trombone lessons, barber shops, and batting practices. Lunchtime becomes about as gracious as a pit stop in the Indianapolis 500.

The only meal for which I can count on full attendance is Sunday night supper. Sunday night we break bread in front of the television set with little plastic trays in our laps and improve our minds. Our children would prefer to improve their minds with a "Beverly Hillbillies" rerun, but we always insist upon viewing something educational. Last week while we ate, we were treated to a spectacular documentary presentation of a bull snake swallowing a field mouse.

"Keen! Look at that ol' snake—he isn't even chewing! Isn't that cool, Mom?"

"Cool," I murmured, resolving henceforth to cast my vote with the "Beverly Hillbillies" contingent. Sunday night togetherness may improve our minds, but it doesn't do much for the digestion.

 **August 4**

Today we arrived at Shuswap Lake for three funfilled weeks of "romping across safe, sandy beaches or relaxing in our charming, rustic beach cabin while reveling in the enchant-

If It's Raining

ing vista of acres of pine trees mirrored in crystal-clear waters."

Or something like that. I can't remember the exact wording because our dog ate the brochure last month, but I do recall the picture of the girl in the wee red bikini. She is not romping today. No one romps when it is fifty-eight degrees. In spite of that, my husband is sitting on the porch eagerly peering down the beach, ready to suck in his tummy in case it warms up to romping temperature.

Considering the fact that the windows are glued securely shut with last year's flies, our cabin seems to lean a bit more heavily toward "rustic" than it does to "charming."

I've found that the first four hours in any cabin should be approached with extreme caution and a handful of bandages. During our first four hours, all the doorknobs fell off, the silverware drawer plummeted out and gave me a smart crack on the shin, and the toilet flushed itself continuously with hot water.

The walls of our cabin are done in what the children call "naughty pine" and are adorned with a 1969 calendar, several stern warnings from the management regarding misuse of the plumbing, and a few blobs which look vaguely like A-1 sauce.

But we are delighted to find that there is a complete absence of mosquitoes. In fact, we have it on good authority that there isn't a single mosquito within a five mile radius. It seems that the spiders have eaten them all.

 *August 8*

Today is the fourth d..y of our vacation. The weather is still somewhat of a drawback, there being a lot more of it than we had been bargaining on.

Our biggest problem has been in amusing the children. So far, I have read them three *National Geographics* and one issue of *Business Week* cover to cover, and as of last night I owe our son $2,643 from the Slap Jack tournament.

Today the sun appeared briefly, the shock of which sent five toddlers into hysterics and caused three elderly women to drop to their knees in their Mackintoshes and begin crossing themselves. The rest of us shucked off our foul weather gear, grabbed our suntan oil, and hit the beach at a fast lope, oiling each other's back as we ran. Within ten minutes, however, the sun was swallowed up by clouds and the wind rose to forty miles per hour, immediately swamping two canoes, a water-skiier, and a Donald Duck air mattress.

Since the pilot lights on all the gas space heaters blew out during the gale yesterday afternoon, the inhabitants of all ten cabins met last night for a bonfire on the beach. Unfortunately we mistook a pile of "naughty pine" paneling for the pile of firewood. Our host made a terrible fuss and has flatly refused to light a single pilot light or give out any fresh sheets or towels for the next two weeks. Except for the fact that I dropped a whole bag of marshmallows into the fire and discovered that I was the only one who was old enough to know all the words to "Bye-Bye Blackbird," it was a huge success.

I'm afraid that we are having a bit of difficulty with our bed. Even though it is made out of top quality cornhusks, our mattress sags drastically in the middle, forming a trough which we have dubbed "Death Valley." Unless we lie on our sides and cling tenaciously to the edges, we roll into Death Valley and spend the night eyeball to eyeball, inhaling each other's exhale.

I suppose that I shouldn't complain. The couple in cabin seven have Bunker Hill instead of Death Valley and are forced to lash themselves together with the cord from his bathrobe or risk tumbling out altogether.

 *August 10*

Every newspaper these days features a daily column devoted to horoscopes.

I have often noticed that not only are these daily horoscopes unfailingly optimistic, their character analyses of various birthsigns are invariably flattering.

Based on my experience as a mother—and as an Aries—I've figured basic characteristics which coincide with Zodiac signs.

Aries (March 20—April 19): Individuals born under the sign of Aries tend to be at least eighty-three pounds overweight and prefer the dark meat on a turkey. Basically sedentary, a pair of them make ideal bookends.

Taurus (April 20—May 20): Plagued throughout life by excessive earwax, those born under the sign of Taurus tend to be moody, irritable, and should never eat radishes. Taurus women love having their backs stroked with goose feathers.

Gemini (May 21—June 20): Thanks to the dual nature inherent in Gemini, individuals born under this sign can be counted on always to choose the correct fork at dinner, and to use it to pick their teeth.

Cancer (June 21—July 20): Cancer men are compulsive toenail-biters and invariably wear monogrammed undershirts, as do Cancer women. In fact, the former can be distinguished from the latter only by examining their palms for an outcropping of reddish-brown hair, especially obvious during the full moon.

Leo (July 21—August 22): Never loan your library card to a Leo. These individuals are basically parasites and spend their lives waiting for others to push them through revolving doors.

Virgo (August 23—September 22): Virgo women are known for wearing the same socks for a week and the inability to pronounce the letter "R." Virgo men are given to placing long distance obscene phone calls and reversing the charges.

Libra (September 23—October 22): Libra men are noticeable for their extreme overbite, enabling them to eat a ham sandwich through venetian blinds. Libra women are exceptionally frugal, devoting their entire lives to making evening gowns out of surplus parachutes and knitting their own drapes.

Scorpio (October 23—November 21): Those born under the sign of Scorpio are compulsive thumbsuckers who often suffer from acute dandruff, nervous tension, and yaws. Scorpio women have limpid, intensely beautiful eyes and bad breath.

Sagittarius (November 22—December 21): Sagittarius men are notorious in early life for practical jokes, liking nothing better than to serve twelve-year-old Chivas Regal scotch in a dribble glass. In later life they become convinced that they can walk on water. Sagittarius women suffer from ingrown toenails.

Capricorn (December 22—January 19): Although frequently obsessed by the conviction that wasps have nested in their ears, those born under the sign of Capricorn enjoy simple pleasures and can often be found sitting in a linen closet smelling the clean sheets.

Aquarius (January 20—February 18): Unreliable, pessimistic, and subject to sties, those individuals born under the sign of Aquarius religiously eschew rough language, although a certain Aquarian was overheard to say "Darn it, anyhow" shortly after having been disemboweled by an enraged grizzly.

Pisces (February 19—March 20): Men born under the sign of Pisces are easily recognizable by their low foreheads, pendulous earlobes, and their inability to pronounce "aluminum." Pisces women are inordinately proud of their hair. No one knows why.

August 11

I know a couple named Bert and Brenda who spend the entire summer exploring side roads, the little tree-lined byways that most of us pass at fifty miles per hour while murmuring "We simply *must* take that road one of these days and see where it goes."

Actually I rarely pass these charming byways unless my

gas gauge needle has just stopped quivering at a point roughly a quarter of an inch below empty. And it seems that every time I have gasoline, I am either escorting fifteen Cub Scouts on an educational tour of the local filtration plant or speeding toward the emergency ward with a child who has just lopped off an ear.

Bert and Brenda have no children, which leaves them relatively free to amble about the countryside discovering waterfalls, staying in quaint country inns which charge two dollars a night and include a three-course breakfast, and picking up ten-piece antique maple dining-room suites for $3.37.

The only likely-looking country side road I've ever explored turned out to be a farmer's driveway where I was met by three half-starved German Shepherds, one of whom ate my license plate. And no matter what the farmer said, he didn't even *own* a prize laying hen. Especially not the one I ran over.

It is, of course, entirely possible that Bert and Brenda have had similar unpleasant experiences while exploring side roads. In fact, I shouldn't be at all surprised if every third trip or so was a kidney-jolting journey to a dump. But, being childless, they can keep mum about the whole messy affair, which is a bit difficult to do when your son insists on taking a dead chicken to school for Show-and-Tell.

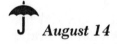 *August 14*

Since we have spent ten days here at the lake so far, we are enjoying a bit of seniority over the newcomers. They allow us to use the best ping-pong paddles and to chop all the firewood for the bonfires.

Our feud with the management broadened in scope last week as a certain *esprit de corps* developed among cabins one through ten. The main contention, you may remember, arose over management's refusal to light the pilot lights on the gas heaters or to supply clean linen and towels.

Our delegate from cabin two informed management that unless heat was forthcoming, concerted retaliatory action would be taken in the form of flushing great wads of paper towels and potato parings into his septic tank.

Management capitulated immediately; between the combined aromas of fresh linen and gas fumes, everyone is walking around in a state of euphoria.

Yesterday I discovered that our son has been wearing his "favorite" socks all week. Though admittedly unhygienic, it has helped cut down on visits to the laundromat.

Finally the weather improved sufficiently to allow a bit of waterskiing. Waterskiing is a lot like patting your head while rubbing your stomach; it looks easy when someone else does it. I could never finish murmuring the litany "skis up, knees bent, feet together, rope held to chest" before someone yelled "Hit it!" and I found myself face down, blearily gazing at the beer bottles on the bottom of the lake while the skis beat great welts in the region of my shoulderblades.

Took the children to a drive-in movie last night at a nearby small town. During the day, a local farmer grazes fifty head of Black Angus at the Starlight Drive-in. A trip to the concession stand in the dark was like walking over a mine field. It was quite an entertaining show starring a little girl named Jane Withers who bears a striking resemblance to Josephine the Plumber. Unfortunately they had lost the last reel, but they showed the first reel twice to make up for it.

Eric feel asleep on the way home, and I sneaked his "favorite" socks off. I had planned to wash them and drape them over the gas space heater, but the pilot light just blew out again.

 *August 17*

In spite of it being a supposedly uplifting TV show, I find that whenever I watch "The Waltons," I invariably become depressed.

The sad fact of the matter is that our family is nowhere near as well adjusted as the Waltons. "Rats," I mutter every time I view the show. "There they are, poverty-stricken, victims of the Great Depression, struggling to wrench a meager existence out of the unyielding soil. Some people have all the luck."

I was determined to simulate the Waltons' spirit of family cooperation, their sense of participation, and by so doing to acquire their unfailing cheerfulness. First I concentrated on my son, Eric-boy, who was lying on the floor reading an issue of *Pop Music Today.*

"How're them chores comin', Son?"

"What chores?" he asked, looking at me as if I had suddenly begun speaking in tongues.

"Um, well, there's the butter," I mumbled.

"The butter?" he repeated, obviously mystified. Actually, I don't churn butter. And taking one pound of butter out of its paper and putting it on the butter dish isn't much of a chore.

"Have you fed the livestock?" I asked.

"You mean him?" he replied, pointing to Rover-boy who was absently munching a couple of bearer bonds. Just then his sister came home.

"Did you git them potatoes for me at Ike's on your way home?" I asked.

"No, I got them at the A&P. They give stamps."

"Well, let's git to it and russle up some grub," I chortled, sweeping her off into the kitchen. "You peel the spuds."

I think that there is a possibility of acquiring the Waltons' spirit of family cooperation and sense of participation. All we have to do is discover how to peel a box of instant mashed potatoes.

 *August 19*

I am convinced that everyone is born with either a Number Mind or a Word Mind.

Number Minds go through life nonchalantly splitting infinitives and inferring when they should be implying. Those of us with Word Minds have to take off our shoes to add nine and eight.

Now I would never read mathematical puzzles were they not written in Words; I read "Fun with Figures" for the same reason I read the financial page, which, though completely unintelligible, is full of glorious Words like "optimum capital allocation" and "unprecedented maximization."

Yesterday's mathematical puzzle featured the following folksy dialogue:

"What's that label on our garage, Dad?" Alan asked. "It's a funny number anyway."

Dad smiled. "The building permit number," he replied. "What's funny about it?"

The boy grinned. "It's just four less than a seventh of what you get if you square its last three digits."

You figure it out.

Number Minds will undoubtedly convert that gay repartee into an equation and completely ignore the obvious pathos of the situation. There is Dad, just off the 6:20 train, wanting nothing more than five minutes alone in his vibrator chair.

Before he can get into the house, Alan, whom I envisage as an adenoidal twelve-year-old, and probably a bedwetter to boot, leaps out from behind the privet hedge and starts whining, "What's that label on our garage? It's a funny number anyway."

Dad, admirably restraining his immediate impulse to tell Alan to button his lip, smiles and explains. But instead of leaving well enough alone, he asks Alan what's so darn funny.

Alan chuckles (adenoidally) and begins to spout his nonsense about four less a seventh to poor Dad (plainly a Word Mind like me who gave up trying to balance his checkbook sixteen years ago).

The whole situation is almost as depressing as the financial page.

If It's Raining

One of the fallacies of summer holidays is that you are going to get some serious reading done while you are lying on the beach.

Our house is full of volumes of Thackeray and Dickens in genuine, gold-leaf binding—really solid stuff that I've always meant to read but never have.

There is always the temptation to tuck one of these literary classics into the beach bag between the earplugs and the swim fins. What better time for communing with Tolstoy, you reason, than while you're basking idly beside the sea for seven whole days?

In the first place, Russian novels are out. Russian names are difficult enough to keep track of when you're sitting by yourself on a snowy Thursday afternoon. They become completely hopeless to sort out while your toes are being nibbled by sand fleas and a small girl is busily swatting the mosquitoes on your back with her Eskimo Pie.

If you will notice, used bookstores in resort areas invariably stock at least twenty-eight volumes of *War and Peace* with sand in the bindings that vacationers are determined not to lug all the way back to Des Moines again. I am not sure what the local residents do with that much Tolstoy, but by September they undoubtedly have enough to build themselves a dandy seawall.

No, for the beach you want something light and airy. The instruction manual for an electric coffeemaker is ideal. For variety you might include the washing directions for your husband's swim trunks or the label on the bottle of insect repellent.

Let's fact it, rather than reading anything, you will undoubtedly spend most of your summer holiday peering myopically in the direction of the water and wondering whether your son is the blond head bobbing fifty yards off shore or the boy who is scuttling along the beach waving the top half of someone's bikini.

☂ *August 21*

Today, on the seventeenth day of our vacation on Shuswap Lake, we were informed that for almost three weeks we have been drinking unpurified lake water.

I had suspected as much when I found snails in the bottom of a pitcher of lemonade, but the rest of the family carried on as if Shuswap Lake was fed by the Hudson River. They immediately blamed the water supply for every complaint they've had since we arrived, from intestinal afflictions to heel blisters.

This morning I took the children horsebackriding. We were greeted at the corral by a man who I'm sure was Chill Wills. His upper plate was clacking so alarmingly that I couldn't understand much of what he said except "Howdy, Ma'am" and "Two dollars an hour each in advance." While the children were assisted onto two gentle mares, I found myself being heaved aboard a vicious looking sorrel who was chewing the bit and obviously wishing that it was a human ankle bone.

"You'll like 'Perdition.' He's got spunk," Chill Wills clacked at me.

"Spunk, my foot! He has rabies!" I replied as we left for what I truly believed to be the Last Roundup.

Soon we reached a gentleman's agreement; Perdition would stumble along gnashing his huge yellow teeth and frothing at the mouth while I would content myself with clinging to the pommel with both sweaty hands and sobbing.

Alas, disaster struck in the form of a killer butterfly. When it fluttered past Perdition's bloodshot eyes, he gave a strangled scream and bolted across a marsh gibbering pitifully. First I yelled "Whoa!" When that seemed to drive him to even greater frenzy, I switched to "Help! Help!" I finally settled for a steady moan-sob combination, which my children tell me I kept up for an hour after Perdition halted abruptly to eat a patch of poison sumac.

I have the beginnings of an acute discomfort in the lower back, which by tomorrow gives every promise of developing into excruciating agony, should I be so foolish as to attempt to sit down.

But according to my family, Perdition had nothing to do with it; it's all that lake water I drank.

August 29

I recently extended a dinner invitation to friends of mine from New York City, a couple who have an eighteen-month-old son.

I checked with his mother beforehand to find out Bobby's favorite foods.

"Oh, any finger foods will do," she assured me. "Mashed potatoes, creamed carrots, Jell-O . . . "

"I'm afraid that I don't have a high chair," I said.

"That's no problem. We always carry the Manhattan yellow pages around with us. It makes a terrific booster seat. Of course, that's about all it's good for these days. Last Tuesday I went to call an electrician and found out that all the pages have been glued shut with blobs of gravy."

"I haven't had anyone Bobby's age around for a long time," I admitted.

"He's at a super stage," his mother insisted. "He's still too little to pick all the mushrooms out of his spaghetti sauce and roll them up in one corner of the tablecloth. He doesn't have any loose baby teeth dangling over his lower lip and threatening to fall out any minute. And he doesn't report all the revolting things he saw on the sidewalk on the way to school. In fact, he's only got one fault."

"What's that?"

"He's not sure where his mouth is yet. And there's nothing that dampens my enjoyment of coq au vin more than watching him stabbing away at his cheek with a fistful of creamed carrots."

This Must Be the Weekend

August 30

I truly believe that one of the finest aspects of our modern culture is the growing lack of social pressures on a couple to have children.

There are, however, noticeable differences between childless couples and those who have chosen to raise a family.

You know that you are in the home of a couple with children when you find yourselves playing bridge with an Animal Rummy deck;

—When the man of the house refers to his middle toe as "the little piggy that had roast beef";

—When you find yourself drinking a martini out of a Fred Flintstone mug;

—When you ask your hostess whether you can borrow her nail scissors and she simply looks at you and bursts into hysterical laughter.

On the other hand, you know that you must be in the home of a couple who have chosen to remain childless when you can use their bathroom without first removing a toidy seat;

—When the living room contains a white brocade sofa, a glass-topped coffee table, and sixteen current affairs magazines with the covers on;

—When your host informs you that he has *volunteered* to act as leader for a Cub Scout pack;

—When you notice that there is no lock on their bedroom door;

—When you discover that they don't know the location of the emergency ward at the local hospital.

☂ September 8

I have to admit that I'm overjoyed that my children are back in school.

Don't misunderstand me; I like my children. But I like them in their place. Unfortunately, their place closes down for two months every summer.

While the first day of summer vacation is taken up with whooping "No more pencils, no more books, no more teacher's dirty looks" and feeding their geography notes to the dog, by mid-afternoon of the second day both children are reduced to lying under the dining room table and whining "There's nothing to *do!*"

"What do you mean, 'there's nothing to do'? Just look at your room!" is met with stony silence. (Mothers, it must be admitted, are not overly sympathetic toward people who have nothing to do. It is a callous attitude acquired in the process of folding diapers with one hand while stirring chocolate pudding with the other.)

I confess to being a bit out of sorts as well. Not only has my consciousness-raising session been canceled for the summer, but I must remember to close the bathroom door again.

As the summer progresses, my children seek out others with whom to mope. They follow me around the house like a Greek chorus, watching me dust.

While I am grateful to acknowledge the end of summer, I pride myself on the fact that I did adapt. I learned not only to live with a refrigerator full of Kool-Aid and a kitchen floor liberally sprinkled with granulated sugar, but I even occasionally yielded to the temptation to surreptitiously hoof my way through a chorus or two of "Me and My Shadow" while peeling potatoes.

Fortunately, last month the children were too caught up in the heady decision of whether to buy two-hole or three-hole filler paper to notice that the flush of excitement that had begun rising to my cheeks in late August was something more than simply hot flashes.

The children's annual return to school signifies a further step in their educational experience, a continuation of the emotional and intellectual awakening process so vital to maturity.

It also means that I can again go to the bathroom without closing the door and watch "As the World Turns" instead of "The Three Stooges."

Since their return to school, the children have displayed a great deal of solicitous concern as to my psychological welfare, suddenly bereft of their company as I am.

Of course it would never do to let the children know that I am simply ecstatic that they have returned to school.

"I'll bet you miss those great Monopoly games we had in July. I'll bet nobody ever played Monopoly for forty-seven hours before," my son sighed.

"And remember the time we went to the beach and that fat little kid dropped his Eskimo Pie on your stomach?" his sister added.

"Mom's lucky, though. We have to go to school every day, but she can still watch 'The Three Stooges' every afternoon."

"Somehow it isn't the same program without you," I assured him.

"Sure must be dull around home these days."

"Yeah," I sighed blissfully. "Sure is dull."

September 9

While a cat or a dog is usually considered a family pet, a child may beg for something in a cage or a bowl to keep on his bureau as his very own.

As a public service for mothers (who invariably will be obliged to feed these pets, clean their cages, and pick cedar shavings out of the child's underwear drawer), I present the following Child's Garden of Pets:

The Turtle: Isn't he tiny? See him swim? See him sun himself? He does everything but eat. Have you tried dried flies? Have you tried lettuce? Have you tried hot pastrami?

The Hamster: Isn't he cunning? Watch him store food in his cheek pouches. My he smells odd! See him run around in his exercise wheel? He does that all day long. He does it all *night* long, too. I've *tried* oiling the wheel. Let's put his cage in the basement behind the woodpile.

Tropical Fish: Aren't they lovely colors? No, you can't kiss them. They are very delicate. They live in a special $12.98 tank with a $17.50 heating element, a $14.95 pump which uses granulated charcoal and a fiberglass filter, and we put algae retardant in their water and feed them brine shrimp eggs. No, I don't know *why* they are all floating upside down.

The Parakeet: Aren't his feathers a pretty shade of blue? They match the rug so well. Isn't that handy? Let's teach him how to sit on our finger. Where are all those bandages I bought last Tuesday?

The Mice: Mommy mouse is pregnant. Isn't that nice? She has six darling little babies. No, I don't know why Daddy mouse ate them. Maybe they made too much noise and jumped on their beds.

The Snake: Yes, he's very pretty. Yellow and black are *my* favorite colors, too. I'm sure that he's not a bit slimy. No, I don't want to hold him!

The Chameleon: Did you know that he changes the color of his body to match his background? Isn't he clever? That is called protective coloration. It makes it very hard for his enemies to see . . . Well, don't just sit there, look for him!

J *September 11*

As much as it might seem that way, mothers are not with their children every minute of the day.

Consequently, all manner of things go on that mother never knows about. Which is undoubtedly all for the best.

You must impress on the children that you'd just as soon not know that Susie is blowing bubbles in her Ovaltine again, but if she is sitting on the living room floor drinking Mr. Clean, you'd like to be told.

When the children misbehave, threatening them with "Wait until your father comes home" is not a particularly good idea, as this tends to make Daddy about as popular as Atilla the Hun, and the children will await his homecoming with the same degree of enthusiasm as they do a flu shot.

Besides, Daddy is apt to be unreliable. After a particularly irksome day of watching the Dow Jones averages go down and feeling his collar trying to strangle him, Daddy may regard the fact that Marvin ate $6.98 worth of artificial fruit as being vaguely amusing. Marvin, sensing a potential ally, makes Daddy a nice, strong drink, leaps onto his lap and begins stroking his cheek, leaving you brandishing half of a wax banana and demanding, "Well, what are you going to *do* about it?"

Since you are destined to be both judge and jury, you must remember the cardinal rule: *Never punish a child when you are angry.*

If you have gone all white around the mouth and are seeing red flashes, it's probably just as well to lock yourself in the bathroom, where you can howl, stomp your feet, and hold your breath until you turn blue. When the child knocks on the

If It's Raining

door and asks if you are ready to punish him, put your mouth to the keyhole and yell, "Not yet, dear. If I touch you, I might kill you."

In an hour or so you will find that you're calm, and the child is out in the sandbox making a castle. Go to him. Smile and say, "I'm not angry any more, Bobby. Now I'm going to whale the tar out of you!"

September 16

I never was a hypochondriac. Unless I was faced with evidence to the contrary, I always assumed that my spleen and pancreas were in there somewhere, plugging away at whatever they were supposed to be doing.

But last week we bought a life insurance policy. And instead of giving us another desk calendar or an ice pack, which we really could have used, our insurance agent presented us with a copy of the *Family Medical Encyclopedia*, a frank discussion of 2,400 medical subjects from *Abasia* to *Zymurgy*.

Now I'm not in favor of censorship in principle. But I do believe that certain types of literature are best kept out of the hands of impressionable people. Like me.

When my husband arrived home from work tonight, I was lying in the dark on the living room sofa. Across my forehead was a homemade ice pack (twenty-seven ice cubes tied in a hockey sock).

"What's the matter?" he asked.

"Agranulocytosis," I whispered.

"What's that again?"

"Agranulocytosis," I repeated. "Also called malignant leukopenia. A rare but often fatal disease in which the bone marrow is affected and the manufacture of essential white

This Must Be the Weekend   121

blood cells is severly diminished."

"You've been reading that darned *Medical Encyclopedia* again," he said accusingly, pointing to the well-thumbed book which lay, disease-down, across my knees. "Three days ago you were positive that you had scurvy just because your gums were bleeding."

"So I forgot that I had bought a new toothbrush. But this time I'm sure. In the first place I have a high fever and ulcerations in my mouth. Look," I said, pointing to my upper lip.

"That's a cold sore. What's for dinner?"

It's impossible to get any sympathy around here. I don't know how he can expect me to make dinner when I can't even make white blood cells.

 *September 18*

I have always been amazed that for one woman "cleaning house" is a task to which she devotes forty-five minutes a week, while for another woman the job is literally full time, demanding at least eight hours a day.

Oddly enough, both houses look equally presentable.

I have recently devised a theory to explain this phenomenon: household dirt is composed of three layers. The first woman cleans only layer one; the second cleans all three layers.

Layer One: This layer is composed of highly visible effluvia, usually sticky. In this category is the blob of grape jelly on the stereo, the orange juice on the kitchen floor, the dab of French's mustard on the telephone, and the two cigarette butts stuck in the rubber plant. Also included in this category are items temporarily misplaced, such as the tube of denture adhesive on the piano, the empty ice-cube tray on the coffee table, and the living bra draped over the toaster.

Layer Two: Also known as the Twilight Zone, it consists

of things you don't see unless you are down on your hands and knees looking for a cufflink. In this category is the tumbleweed of dust under the bed, the wad of chewing gum stuck to the back leg of the end table, and the beef bone buried behind the dresser. Many items considered hopelessly lost, such as library cards, tweezers, and the meat thermometer, are often lurking in Layer Two.

Layer Three: Layer Three is composed solely of things no one ever sees except mothers-in-law. It includes the four dog biscuits under the refrigerator, the dust on the tops of the drapes, the dried carrot stick stuffed behind the books in the bookcase, the price tags on the tops of the paintings, and the three obscene books tucked behind the spare blanket on the top shelf of the linen closet.

September 21

A popular women's magazine recently ran a test whereby the reader could determine her degree of assertiveness.

Each question presented a situation, your response to it showing whether you normally react in an aggressive, assertive, or passive manner.

Being masochistically addicted to personality quizzes, I endeavored to answer the following:

A friend asks you to accept a gift you do not want. You . . .

1. Accept the gift but indicate you don't really want it;

2. Thank your friend but explain that you cannot accept this gift;

3. Do not accept the gift.

Now, the major problem with this situation is that absolutely no hint is given of the type of gift that she offered. I mean, is it something small and intimate that I could simply tuck away on the top shelf of the linen closet, and later assure my friend that I was indeed using and/or wearing it? Or is it something three feet high at the shoulders with drooping jowls that will leak all over the new broadloom?

Your husband has been throwing his clothes all over the bedroom during the past week. You . . .

1. Put up with the mess as best as you can;

2. Tell him you would appreciate it if he would try to keep his clothes hung up;

3. Pick up the clothes because you want to help him.

Again, no hint is given as to *why* he threw his clothes all over the bedroom. No mention was made of what, if anything, I was doing with my own clothes. From everything I've been reading lately, a moderate amount of marital clothes-throwing is a good thing.

And it is a lot more fun than sitting around taking personality quizzes.

 *September 28*

The person who said "Neither a borrower nor a lender be" didn't live five miles from the nearest supermarket.

Suburbanites shop but once a week. As I know of no one who is able to accurately predict his family's dietary whimsies over a seven-day period, between Tuesday and Friday of each week we are invariably found running between each other's houses carrying measuring cups.

Not only is the communal sharing of nature's bounty an expression of true humanitarian spirit, but it enables one to avoid the dilemma of making baking powder biscuits without baking powder.

Most of the neighborhood borrowing is confined to such temporary culinary short-falls as an egg, a small onion, or a cup of Vermouth. One woman, however, is notorious for stretching the bonds of Christian charity.

"How can anybody 'borrow' a standing rib roast?" I grumbled to one of my friends.

"You lent Joyce a roast?!?" my friend Alice exclaimed, aghast.

"Don't be ridiculous. What would I be doing with a standing rib roast? Fortunately she settled for three pounds of hamburger."

"You have to understand about Joyce," Alice explained. "I love the woman like I do my own sister, but she has never caught on to our system. No matter what she borrows, she always returns sugar."

"Sugar?"

"She figures everyone uses sugar, and it's simpler than remembering what she originally borrowed. Besides, she enjoys watching the expression on the bag boy's face every week when she buys 137 pounds of sugar."

☂ *October 1*

To me, an autumn afternoon has always been a magic time, a time for a romantic stroll through a carpet of crisp, golden leaves, while the sun turns my hair to a burnished halo, and a cool breeze whispers a sad farewell to a waning summer.

To my husband, an autumn afternoon means lying on the sofa with a bowl of pistachios on his chest and watching six straight hours of football.

I suppose that there's nothing to prevent me from taking a romantic walk through carpets of crisp, golden leaves by myself. But bashing around in a pile of leaves alone is hardly romantic. Besides, I can hear the neighbors now: "Look at the Stahl dame, Fred, out there jumping around in a pile of leaves. Get the kids inside while I call the police."

The only alternative seems to be to put a bowl of pistachios on my chest and watch the football game, too. But I regard football games like I do taffy apples and kittens: one is plenty. By 3:30 last Saturday afternoon I had finished my pistachios and darned every sock in the house, including the ones my husband was wearing.

"Let's go play tennis," I suggested brightly, turning off the television set. My husband screamed as if I had driven a stake through his heart.

"The Jets have fourth-and-two on the three-yard line!" he shrieked as he leaped from the sofa. He wrenched the set on,

If It's Raining

only to hear the announcer say, "Well, folks, you just saw probably the most electrifying play in the entire history of professional football."

"No, I didn't!" my husband bawled, pointing at me
accusingly. "She turned the set off!"

"I'm tired of watching football," I complained.

"I'll tell you what. Have you noticed that carpet of crisp,
golden leaves outside?"

"I sure have!" I said, expectantly.

"Why don't you go out and rake them? I'll bet they'd make
a swell compost heap!"

☂ *October 2*

Owning a grandfather clock is one of those mixed blessings like suddenly finding yourself in possession of a harem.
No matter how proud of it you are, from then on getting a good
night's sleep becomes a bit difficult.

The first night that we had the clock, I noticed that my
husband was lying rigidly in bed with one hand on his chest
and appeared not to be breathing. "What's the matter?" I asked
anxiously. "Are you sick?"

"It's my heart. I can *hear* it beating," he whispered in a
stricken voice.

"Relax. It's just Big Ben downstairs."

"How long does this go on?" he demanded. I was tempted
to say "Till the old man dies," but I restrained the impulse.

During the next several hours, Grandfather's Westminster
chimes effectively wrenched us rudely from the verge of sleep
every fifteen minutes, melodiously informing us that it was
quarter-past, half-past, or quarter-till. Grandfather left it up to
us to figure out quarter-past, half-past, or quarter-till *what*. I
suppose that it would have been simple enough for one of us to

get out of bed and look. But getting up involved not only locating slippers but running the risk of finding ourselves wide awake and hungry. Instead, we decided to lie there and wait for the hour to strike.

But invariably, the striking of the hour—which is a veritable pops concert—was the one we dozed through, only to awaken fifteen minutes later to learn that is was once again quarter-past *something*.

The next night we decided to cover Grandfather with an old sheet at night, like we would a touchy parrot. I thought that we had solved the problem nicely until our daughter ran into our room in the middle of the night.

"There's a ghost standing in the downstairs hall," she shrieked, "and I can hear his heart beating."

 *October 6*

It must be fall. Not only are my friends more relaxed because the kids are back in school but I find myself seized with my annual urge to clean under the refrigerator.

I know it's all psychological. When I'm beseiged on every side with the sight and smell of burning leaves and the sounds of muffled activity as robins pack to leave their nest in our chimney for their trek South, I suppose that it's only natural to feel guilty that the part of our nest that lies under the refrigerator hasn't been cleaned for a year.

The best cure that I've found for this fall-time attack of guilt is simply to lie down with my feet up and a cool cloth on my forehead and murmur, "This, too, shall pass." In addition, it helps to ask myself two pertinent questions:

Q: What exactly do you propose to do?

A: I propose to court a severe rupture by attempting to move a three-hundred-pound refrigerator in order to wipe up

128   *If It's Raining*

six ounces of ick that has accumulated underneath it. Unless I succeed regarding the rupture, I then propose to move the refrigerator back so that "ick" can collect underneath it again.

Q: For whom do you propose to do this?

A: Obviously not for my family. My family is concerned only with what is *in* the refrigerator; I could store dead frogs underneath it for all they care. Even if I were to tell them about the hideous job I had cleaning it, and about the rupture and all, the only accolade I could expect from them would be a rather disinterested "Uhhuh," if that.

By the time I have finished answering those two questions, I find that my pangs of conscience have vanished. Better to let another year or two of ick accumulate. By then we'll probably be moving, and the moving men can haul the refrigerator out while I stand poised with a damp cloth, ready to swoop upon the refuse making little "Tsk, tsk, how did *that* get there?" noises. As if I didn't know.

 *October 9*

Every modern child psychology book will tell you that it is important to instill a sense of responsibility in your children.

Tell them that along with the obvious benefits, being a member of a family entails certain obligations on their part. They will express delight at the prospect of being allowed to assume a vital, active role in the family. If they don't exhibit delight, simply threaten to cut off their allowances and leave them out in the forest to be raised by wolves.

No matter how old he is, any child is capable of helping around the house. Different ages have different capabilities.

Children three to five years old are sobbingly eager to help you do everything from baking brownies to putting on your girdle. All they need is a bit of direction.

They can:

1. *Run simple errands.* Just as jet engine manufacturers employ midgets in assembly lines, children this size are invaluable for crawling under beds to determine whether that dark blob is a missing navy blue sock that must be washed or simply a banana skin.

2. *Empty the ashtrays.* At this age, you owe it to your children's sense of responsibility to smoke. How can they empty the ashtrays if you don't smoke? Of course, they will empty half the contents of the ashtray into the paper bag under the sink and the other half onto the kitchen floor, but it's the thought that counts. Besides, the kitchen floor needs washing anyway. Well, doesn't it? Of course it does. It has cigarette ashes all over it.

3. *Put their toys away.* While you are busy filling the ashtrays, your children will be busy emptying the toy box. If they start at 2:00 P.M. picking up the building blocks under the dining room table, the toy cars under the sofa cushions, and the marbles on the stairs, they *may* finish by bedtime. At this rate they will have no time for the ashtrays. On second thought, you'd better stop smoking. Not only will it be better for your lungs, but you won't have to wash the kitchen floor nearly so often.

Children from six to nine lack the enthusiasm exhibited by the three-to-five-year olds, but still can be persuaded to:

1. *Feed their pets.* Unless his pet is vocal enough to meow or bark while pointing to his mouth with one paw, the child may very well forget this chore. It is therefore necessary for you to badger him to feed the goldfish, as the only way the goldfish can remind him is to begin floating belly-side-up in their bowl.

2. *Pick up the dirty clothes and throw them down the laundry chute.* This is one thing that a child really *likes* to do. In fact, he may get so carried away that when he finishes with the dirty clothes, he will begin flinging down all his clean clothes, his baseball cards, the alarm clock—and the cat. This makes for quite a clutter in the basement, not to mention a decidedly neurotic kitty.

If It's Raining

3. *Make their beds*. This involves simply pulling the spread up over all the things he sleeps with; at this age, two teddy bears and a basketball. When questioned, he will argue that since he is going to be getting back into the bed in just twelve hours, having the blanket already turned down and the teddy bears and the basketball in there will save time. Besides, nobody ever sees his room except him, and he likes it that way. Personally, I've never been able to come up with a reasonable argument to refute this logic.

The only solution is to keep the door to his room closed and tell yourself that he will do better as he gets older.

While not necessarily true, it's a consoling thought, rather like imagining that a pastel mink coat would only make you look fat.

Unfortunately, large-sized children (from ten to thirteen) do not have much time for chores. But in the odd moments when they are not practising the bassoon or determining how long it will take an airplane flying six-hundred miles per hour into a fifty-mile per hour headwind to fly from Cedar Rapids to Bombay, they may be induced to:

1. *Mow the lawn*. Regrettably, the only children who are really keen to mow the lawn are middle or little. Letting a middle or little struggle with the lawn mower will cause the neighbors to report you to the welfare authorities as being unfit parents. But by the time a child reaches a size where the neighbors begin to say, "Why doesn't that big lout of a kid next door do any work?" he will be completely disenchanted with the thrill of mowing. He will insist that he is not big enough to mow the lawn and will lop off his big toe just to prove it.

2. *Set and clear the dinner table*. While this may work admirably if your cuisine lends itself to plastic plates and jelly glasses, I would be a bit loath to entrust a handful of heirloom Limoges to anyone who has been known to trip over a piece of lint on the carpet.

3. *Take out the garbage*. To be absolutely safe, it's best to add "and put it into the trash can." If your son is anything like mine, he may very well absentmindedly take the garbage to school and stuff in into his desk until lunchtime, when he will

bring it home and deposit the bag in the kitchen again.

4. *Climb up on the roof and pry the Frisbee out of the chimney.* Of course, if you didn't have a large-sized child, you wouldn't *have* a Frisbee in the chimney. But at this age, a chore is a chore.

☂ *October 12*

I am admittedly an astonishingly gullible person. The following, however, is a list of phrases that even I tend not to believe:

Child: "So what if this is the last turnpike exit for fifty-seven miles. I said I don't have to go."

Husband: "Of course I'm not going to fall asleep. I'm just going to lie here for ten minutes and rest my eyes."

Friends: "Listen, any time you're in the neighborhood, be sure to drop in."

Husband: "He'll grow out of it. He's only two."

Man at the door: "I'm taking a survey in your area."

Husband: "Don't call a repairman. I can fix the toaster blindfolded."

Mother-in-law: "He's still in diapers? I had his father completely trained when he was six months old."

Husband: "He'll outgrow it. He's only seven."

Child: "And I promise that I'll clean his cage every single day."

Neighbor: "There's no hurry to get her neutered. She's not old enough to have kittens."

Husband: "He'll outgrow it. He's only twelve."

Pantyhose package: "One size fits all—95 to 165 pounds."

Husband: "What do you mean, it's six o'clock and you want to stop already? Why, I'm just hitting my stride. Don't

If It's Raining

worry, there will be lots of motels with vacancies at nine o'clock."

Child: "He followed me home."

Husband: "Of course I don't need glasses. It's just that this wise guy publisher is trying to save money by using microscopic print."

Friend: "Take it from me. Soybean futures are nothing but a license to print money."

Husband: "I mean it. I don't want anything for my birthday."

Child: "And I promise that I'll practice an hour every day."

Husband: "He'll outgrow it. He's only eighteen."

☂ *October 14*

In response to several magazine articles exhorting me to enjoy the incomparable autumnal exhilaration of an October picnic, I would like to offer the following first-hand observations:

Granted, there is a crispness in the air when it's twelve degrees above freezing that effectively eliminates the mosquito problem while keeping all the food nicely chilled. Except the lemonade, which inexplicably remains at approximately body temperature and contains a dozen mosquitos who threw themselves in simply to get warm.

Of course, by the time you have finished hauling a picnic hamper, playpen, baseball bat, blanket, radio, four folding chairs, and a cooler that alone weighs more than a four-year-old child to the last empty picnic table (which is invariably located beside the comfort station), you are quite warm, especially under your arms where your woolen sweater has begun to scratch unmercifully.

Within ten minutes a chill northern wind will come whipping through the trees, sending sixteen dried oak leaves into the potato salad, whereupon someone will suggest that we throw the old ball around a bit before eating to get the blood stirring.

Now even though I take care to hold my hand correctly, just before the old ball reaches me I succumb to some primordial urge and throw both hands over my face, crouch with my head between my knees, and begin whimpering. Whereupon the old ball knocks three pounds of potato salad, not to mention sixteen dried oak leaves, into the playpen.

Of course, the one jolly thing about October picnics is that you eat all manner of things that you wouldn't dream of eating at home where you are warm and toasty. Children who normally go all pale and trembly when confronted with a carrot stick at lunch, on an October picnic will proceed not only to down thirteen carrot sticks and six deviled eggs that they find buried in the sand under the picnic cooler, but scrape off and eat all the leafy potato salad from the playpen pad.

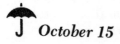 October 15

Dear Mrs. Hall,

I am terribly sorry that I didn't reply sooner to the note you sent me last Tuesday, but I didn't find it until I washed Eric's brown corduroy school pants this morning.

It certainly was a long note. By the time the washer finished spinning, I found so many pieces of paper that I had to wash the entire load over again.

I know that it was an important note, too. I mean, what with molding character and teaching long division, you certainly don't have time to write long notes for pleasure. Besides, one piece (the one stuck to a navy blue stretch sock) said "Urgent."

Since it was obviously so important, I picked all the pieces out of the lint filter and off the clothes and tried to put them together. I'm sorry that the school board gives you such inferior paper; most of the note had turned into a sort of slimy goo, even with the machine set on "Gentle." Unfortunately the only piece I could read, besides the one that said "Urgent," said "Show."

The only show I can think of is a school production like the one I made eighteen Bluebell costumes for in 1973. That was the same year I was room mother, cookie chairman for the PTA, and drove six little girls to hula dancing lessons every Tuesday afternoon.

I don't do that sort of thing now, Mrs. Hall. I mean, "for everything there is a season," and between my bursitis and hot flashes, I'm just not in season anymore. It's no great loss, actually; I put all the Bluebell sleeves in backwards.

There is one other possible interpretation, but somehow I can't imagine that you conduct Show-and-Tell in the sixth grade. Of course we know that they still tell. Heaven knows he's told us a lot about you. And I want you to know that we don't believe even half of it.

But if he's showing anything he shouldn't, I certainly hope you'll phone me immediately.

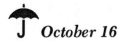 *October 16*

In these times of domestic and foreign turmoil, many readers find themselves unable to decide between the two major political parties. With the election only a few weeks away, the dilemma has become particularly acute. As more and more writers are endeavoring to aid the public in this momentous decision, perhaps it is time to muddy up the waters with my own political observations of how Democrats differ from Republicans.

—When Republicans mention "my club," they mean their country club. Democrats mean Book-of-the-Month Club.

—Republicans get tennis elbow and ulcers. Democrats get heartburn and sties.

—Republicans play golf. Democrats bowl.

—Democrats drive six-year-old green Pontiacs with roof racks. Republicans drive six-month-old Cadillacs with bumper stickers that say "I Like Ike."

—Republicans own horses. Democrats bet on them.

—Republicans drink Drambouie and Cafe Capuchino after dinner. Democrats drink creme de menthe and Sanka.

—Republicans get face lifts and hair transplants. Democrats get nose jobs and silicone implants.

—Republicans have nannies for their children. Democrats have grandmothers.

—Republicans hire good cooks. Democrats marry them.

—Republicans read *Vogue* and the *National Review.* Democrats read *The New Republic* and *Photoplay.*

—Every three weeks, Democratic women make an appointment to have a manicure and get their hair shampooed, cut, and blown dry. So do Republican men.

—Republican men wear monogrammed silk pajamas. Democrats sleep nude.

October 17

In these days of high-pressure salesmanship, an unwary consumer can easily find himself agreeing to purchase unnecessary items. Test your own sales resistance in the following situations:

1. A salesman calls at your door contending that he is taking a survey of selected, intellectually advantaged families in your area. You would:

If It's Raining

(a) Express delight at being part of such an obviously exclusive group. Explain that first you simply must get the garbage cans moved out front or you will miss the pick-up. Ask if he would mind moving the cans while you put on coffee. While he is thus occupied, sneak out the door and go to a movie.

(b) Invite him in, but warn him that the survey will have to be short as you are expecting the exterminator to arrive momentarily to rid the house of lice.

(c) Express relief that he is, in fact, taking a survey, rather than attempting to sell you anything. Confide that you were released from prison last Tuesday after having served six months for setting fire to an encyclopedia salesman.

2. A woman on the telephone informs you that you have won three free dancing lessons. You would:

(a) Express your appreciation and sincere desire to accept her generous offer—if and when you get out of your iron lung.

(b) Laugh heartily. Explain that you have recently been named choreographer for the June Taylor Dancers. Mutter something about "coals to Newcastle."

3. Handling your hair as if it were a particularly revolting strain of tropical fungus, your hairdresser informs you that your whole appearance is drab and lifeless and strongly suggests a forty-five dollar hot oil treatment followed by a color rinse. You would:

(a) Point out to your hairdresser that she's not so great looking herself.

(b) Buy a wig.

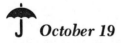 *October 19*

Psychiatrists assure us that fear is normal, that the human animal is beset by one anxiety after another from birth to old age. The following is a catalog of common fears:

A very small child fears that the stopper will come out of his belly-button while he sleeps and that he'll deflate like a beach ball, or that he will fall through the toilet seat and drown.

A twelve-year-old boy is afraid that his teacher will ask him to name the capital of North Dakota.

A girl of twelve is afraid that her classmates will be able to tell that she is wearing a bra. At fourteen, she fears her classmates *won't* be able to tell she is wearing a bra.

A boy of fifteen is afraid that he will fail his algebra test. At nineteen, he fears he'll fail his Wasserman test.

Although people in their twenties are relatively free from anxiety, irrational fears return by age thirty.

A thirty-five-year-old man is afraid that the government will audit his 1976 income tax return, and that someone will erect a motorcycle scrambles track in the vacant lot next door.

At forty-five, he fears that he is the only man in the world who doesn't taper, and that the pain in his arm will turn out not to be tennis elbow, but arthritis.

Women are not free from anxiety during adulthood. A thirty-five-year-old woman is afraid that her son is growing a moustache; a forty-five-year-old is afraid that *she* is growing one.

A forty-year-old woman fears that the lovely green plant her daughter gave her last Mother's Day is really marijuana.

A thirty-year-old woman is afraid that her children will grow up and leave her. A forty-year-old woman is afraid that they *won't*.

☂ *October 20*

All too often, an otherwise memorable dining experience is ruined by the supercilious attitude of a wine steward who appears smugly certain that you wouldn't know Chateau Rothschild from Sunsweet Prune Juice.

It is necessary to intimidate such an individual immediately.

Shake your head wistfully over the wine list, flick a forefinger deprecatingly at three or four items, and sigh "a passable selection. Barely passable. But none of my favorites."

"What wine would you desire?" the steward, who is clearly nonplussed, will stammer.

"For one, Chateau Beaulieu, 1943."

"Chateau Beaulieu?"

"That amusing Tuscany wine. Surely you've heard of it?" Of course the steward hasn't, as you just made the name up on the spot, but he'd sooner swallow his key than admit it.

"Ah, monsieur," he will sigh. "We served our last bottle an hour ago." Extract a small leather notebook from your pocket. Murmer sadly, "no Chateau Beaulieu. What a pity," as you inscribe a large check mark.

The steward will beg to be allowed to bring a bottle of their finest wine.

Eventually he will get around to uncorking it and pouring some into your glass. Ignore it. After two minutes gaze at the glass speculatively, as if wondering how it got there. Raise it to the light. Squint at the color. Raise one eyebrow skeptically. Inhale the bouquet (or whatever it is one is obliged to inhale). Bring the glass slowly to your lips, allowing no more than one teaspoon of liquid to enter your mouth. Do not swallow. Let it just sort of sit there in a puddle on your tongue for twenty seconds, then close your eyes and slowly slosh it over your bridgework.

Sigh deeply and admit that while acceptable, even vaguely amusing, it's no Chateau Beaulieu, 1943.

 *October 21*

Faced with the prospect of inflation, it seems that food is the only flexible item in our household budget.

After all, even though my daughter is so low on school supplies that she has to submit an in-depth report on dealing with the social customs of New Zealand aborigines written on paper towels from the girls' washroom, I can't simply write a letter to the trust company and lop ten dollars off the October mortgage payment.

And I have discovered through bitter experience that the electric company becomes extremely petulant when they receive a whimsical note stating "I.O.U. 357 kilowatts."

As children are notoriously undiscriminating, I expected no resistance to my recently instituted Culinary Austerity Program.

"Why," my son sighed last night, while staring pensively at the chicken leg I had fashioned out of ground beef, "do we always have to have hamburger?"

"What do you mean 'hamburger'?" I countered. "That looks like a chicken leg to me."

"Watch." He picked up his chicken leg, which fell apart in his hand.

"O.K., Smarty," I retorted. "But five nights a week isn't 'always.' Besides, it's not as if I always fix it the same way. What about the hamburger kabobs, the roast suckling hamburger, not to mention the hamburger slice with raisin sauce?"

"How can I forget?" he shuddered. "Why don't we ever have steak any more?"

"As a matter of fact, we *are* having steak tomorrow night."

"Wonderful!" he whooped. "What kind? Porterhouse? Sirloin? T-bone?"

"Salisbury."

 *October 22*

One of the sad facts of my life is that there are not many things which I do well.

But if there is ever an Olympic event to determine proficient sleeping, I am certain to be awarded at least a bronze medal.

I am always amazed at people who declare that once they wake up in the morning, they are completely unable to go back to sleep. One of the chief joys of my life lies in waking up and going back to sleep every fifteen minutes from 6:00 A.M. to 7:30 A.M. In fact, were it not for pressing commitments, I could conceivably drift in and out of consciousness every fifteen minutes until it was time to peel the potatoes for dinner.

Once up, my proclivity for sleep does not diminish. Whenever I attempt to read anything to do with the Boer War, the balance-of-payments deficit, or any type of poetry written in blank verse, my eyes glaze, my chin drops to my chest, and I take on all the alluring charm of an old man on a park bench.

Bus rides never fail to render me half-comatose. Eight stops before I must get off, my eyelids become leaden. Four stops before mine, I must begin biting the sides of my cheeks and driving my fingernails viciously into the palms of my hands to stay awake, a process which gives me the alarming appearance of one who is about to go off into some sort of violent seizure.

Two seconds before the bus reaches my stop, my subconscious wrenches me awake and I leap up, begin yanking feverishly at the bell, and bellowing "Now! ME! Off!"—thus confirming my fellow-passengers' suspicions that they are sharing transportation with one who, far from being a bronze-medal winner, is dangerously deranged.

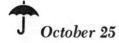 *October 25*

While there is a growing tendency in this country for a couple to limit the number of children they have to only one, I feel that there are several distinct advantages to having two

A younger child is perfectly suited to acquire that size two, fur-trimmed Eskimo parka that set you back $47.98. In fact, with a modest degree of foresight in buying unisex clothing and an unlimited amount of iron-on patches, one needn't buy the second child a stitch until he is sixteen or so.

Remember, too, that if one child is ill, there is always a healthy one to throw into the breech should the trash want taking out or the dog need to be walked.

Besides, two children create a nice balance in the family.

Rather than having to face the tedious frustration of constantly having to function in a solely adult world, a brother or sister proves to be a valuable ally, a cohort in the magical world of make-believe, a partner who will join him in unraveling the mysteries of childhood. Someone to help him pour Ovaltine down the hot air register.

Occasionally, a certain degree of sibling rivalry is bound to occur. Although this is an integral part of their social development, a parent wonders when to step in. While it is definitely advisable to interfere before one child performs a frontal lobotomy on the other with the electric frying pan, it is equally permissible to interfere simply because you are rapidly reaching the point of braining *both* of them with the electric fry pan, just to get a little peace and quiet.

October 27

This is the time of year when I truly envy people who live on farms.

How jolly it must be to stomp out into the back forty in search of your own Halloween pumpkin. Especially since, with a bit of forethought, you can manage to have forgotten to plant any, thus relieving yourself of the bother of finding a round one, not to mention the loathsome duty of gutting it.

If It's Raining

For us city-folk, pumpkins are like Christmas trees; they grow in supermarkets. Ideally, one should prop a prospective jack-o'-lantern up on a stack of canned lima beans and walk around it for ten minutes or so, determining what potential, if any, it has. Unfortunately, by the time I reached the pumpkin display last week, the entire contents of a half-gallon carton of butter pecan ice cream had begun dribbling down my left arm, and I involuntarily grabbed an orange football which gave distinct promise of falling over at 7:00 P.M. Halloween night and setting the verandah on fire.

When I arrived home, I placed the pumpkin on the kitchen counter. As the four of us watched, it toppled over into the butter dish. "*Anyone* can have a plain old *round* pumpkin!" I asserted.

"Anyone but us," my husband observed glumly.

While the children ran outside to tell all the neighbors how their pumpkin mashed the butter, my husband began carving the face. Half an hour later the children returned to survey their father's efforts.

"Keen!" declared our daughter. "But what's all that red stuff in the eye hole!"

"Blood," snarled Daddy, licking the stump of his left thumb.

"Daddy bled all over our punkin!" she wailed.

"Don't worry," I assured her. "Nobody will notice in the dark."

"I've got a suggestion," said my husband. "How about we forget the whole thing next year and just put up our Christmas decorations early?"

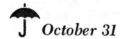 *October 31*

When I was little, Halloween costumes never posed much of a problem. If you couldn't afford to be a storebought skeleton, you simply grabbed the top sheet off your bed and went as a ghost.

These days, children start agonizing in January over their Halloween costumes. And they never want to be anything simple. By November, they generally have it narrowed down to going as either the Marquis de Sade or a typewriter, either of which is a bit of a challenge to whip up out of crepe paper.

One year I decided to enter into the spirit of the season and dress up as a witch. I bought a grotesque rubber mask, a black wig, and wrapped myself in a pair of gangrenous green drapes. Our first caller was a three-year-old, out for the first time. After one look at me, he wet his Donald Duck costume and ran straight home, quacking all the way.

Aside from the costume problem, there's the question of what type of candy to give out. I've learned to buy good quality candy. Otherwise, if there is a blizzard on Halloween night, you may be stuck with 375 of those horrid chewy caramels wrapped in orange paper and end up paying $78.50 to get your bridgework rebuilt.

I must admit that I dislike Halloween intensely. I mean, it took me six weeks and $7.68 worth of heavy-duty aluminum foil to turn my son into the Tin Woodman of Oz. (Actually, he looked more like a leftover meatloaf, but I would cut my tongue out before I told him so.) And for what? Sixteen circus peanuts, fifty-seven pieces of candy corn, and three Chiclettes which I belatedly discovered were actually Feen-a-mint.

Of course, on Halloween night I myself am always wildly extravagant until 7:30, when I realize that I have only three Kraft caramels left. From 7:30 to 7:45 I part with three slices of Italian salami, five dimes, and eleven anchovy olives. At 8:00 I am reduced to either turning out the porch light or distributing a roll of Tums.

The only person I know who avoids this problem is our dentist. Realizing that giving out candy would strike people as being decidedly self-serving, our dentist chooses instead to distribute toothbrushes.

While many youngsters grumble over this heresy, my children profess delight. My son even went so far as to announce to the dentist that he had never had his own toothbrush.

"You told him *what?*" I gasped.

"Well, you didn't want me to hurt his feelings, did you?"

By 10:00 the children had finished their circus peanuts, candy corn, and (unfortunately) their Feen-a-mint. Announcing that they were ready for bed, they grimaced widely to show me their sparkling teeth.

"I even brushed the dog's teeth!" my son confided.

"Not with your new toothbrush?!"

"Of course not. I used yours."

J *November 1*

One of the difficulties with the original concept of equality for women was the fact that the woman who viewed homemaking as a viable career was regarded as either dangerously subversive or mentally deficient.

"Why should anyone," the argument ran, "disdain the inherent challenge of executive decision making in favor of defrosting the refrigerator?"

Those in the vanguard of The Movement neglected to point out that few of us, men or women, ever succeed in scaling the corporate heights. For sheer managerial autonomy, nothing equals the role of homemaker. As there is no higher-up to whom she must report, the homemaker enjoys complete freedom in such situations as the following:

1. The living room windows are covered over with a nasty, yellowish-brown film in which someone has traced the words "Wash me." The homemaker can: (a) Clean the windows with paper towels soaked in ammonia and water; (b) wipe them with a vinegar solution and bath towels; or (c) draw the drapes.

2. Someone has given her a bright magenta sweater with orange reindeer on it. After searching carefully, the homemaker can find no washing instructions. She can: (a) Wash the sweater by hand separately in cold-water soap, roll it gently in

a bath towel, and blow it dry with her hair-dryer; or (b) boil it for ten minutes, then throw it over the hedge to dry.

J *November 2*

Last week our son announced that he was bringing home a "Very Important New Friend."

That afternoon I met them at the door wearing my best Mother-of-the-Year-type smile, waving a batch of home-burned peanut butter cookies. Before he left, I even recited "Casey at the Bat" and gave him my autograph.

The next morning, New Friend arrived to walk to school with Eric.

"Is that your mother?" he gasped, pointing to a lump of frayed terry cloth attached to a cup of reheated coffee.

"Yep," answered Eric.

"She sure looks different in the morning!"

"That's because of her face. She isn't wearing it."

After they left, I ran to the bathroom and peered at myself through the toothpaste specks on the mirror. The regulation number of eyes, lumpy nose, prominent ears, all stared back at me. Actually, I look much the same as I did at twenty. It just takes longer.

I got my lipstick and dug around in the nearly-empty tube with a bobby pin. Rats. This meant a trip to the cosmetic department.

Later that morning, after skulking around the shoe department for an hour, I got up enough courage to approach the lipstick counter, feeling like a candidate for a complexion improvement test. The salesgirls saw me coming and quickly drew straws. A striking redhead undulated over to me, crumpling a very short straw in her fist.

"May I help you?" she asked in a pitying voice.

"I'd like a lipstick."

"What color would you like?"

"Red would be nice," I suggested.

"Let's see, coral would only make you look more sallow," she mused, then suddenly she gasped and began wringing her hands. "We haven't been using our night cream!"

"But when we use our night cream, our husband sleeps on the sofa," I protested.

"Ah, but this night cream is extracted from the tail feathers of male Himalayan bald eagles and is guaranteed nongreasy," she crowed.

"Our husband will be so happy," I murmured. Before I got away, we had spent two weeks' grocery money on enough creams, oils, and extracts to assure the immediate extinction of Himalayan bald eagles. At least we got a lipstick. Unfortunately she gave us Certainly Coral by mistake. It does make us look even more sallow, but when one can recite "Casey at the Bat" like we can, no one really cares.

☂ November 5

Ignoring the outraged screams of our next door rose fetishist, we bought a dog last year. His mother was a pedigreed poodle. Judging from her son's present physique, the putative father must have whinnied.

When we first saw Adolf he was six weeks old, furry, wet-nosed, and cuddly. The fact that his feet were five inches in diameter and he cost $1.50 should have warned us that he would grow up to be a "Big."

We attributed his owner's hysterical joy as we left to his elation that Adolf was going to a good home. I know now that it was shameless relief that he finally unloaded his canine Quasimodo.

After arriving home, Adolf immediately sized up the situation. Taking the lay of the land, he sniffed every chair, table, bed and chest, then squatted on the Oriental carpet and christened it. Satisfied that he had thus made our casa his casa, he crawled into the lazy susan and went to sleep beside the potato chips.

While I blotted up his Mark, my husband went out and bought a $10.98 wicker bed and a large bottle of vinegar. (To those who are uninitiated, applying vinegar to carpeting neutralizes previous indiscretions.)

One hour later, we confidently put Adolf into his wicker bed and called it a night. Before I could turn out the light, Adolf was howling like a banshee. He was trembling violently, obviously miserable and terrified. Not realizing that I had witnessed a performance that qualified for an academy award, I did what all mothers do; I brought him into bed with us "just for tonight."

Every day for four months I would follow Adolf around the house, ready to scoop him up as soon as he started to squat. I'd rush outside with my leaking dog, and if he had any left for the lawn, I'd praise him as if he'd meant to go there all along.

At the end of five months, Adolf was seventy pounds heavier. His errors were of heroic proportions. The Oriental carpet was a mildewed marshland of vinegar. One memorable day, however, he lugged his ponderous bulk to the door and smugly barked his desire to go out. Our neurotic child was trained. Victory was ours.

Now if I can just get him out of our bed.

November 6

Few magazine articles annoy me quite so much as those entitled "How We Manage Our Money," featuring young couples like Babsie and Pudge and their four offspring who get along beautifully on Pudge's salary of $412.76 a month.

I would simply ignore these bits of folklore completely, if my husband didn't insist upon taping them to the bathroom mirror and complaining "What do you *do* with all our money?" possibly implying that I smother it with A-1 Sauce and have it for lunch.

In reading the article, one discovers that Babsie and Pudge pay $128 a month for a twenty-two-room Georgian mansion with hand-hewn beams which was once Millard Fillmore's carriage house. They discovered it one crisp autumn afternoon while tramping through the New England countryside searching for musket balls.

"Certainly it needs work," cried farsighted Babsie, plunging her thumb through the rotten siding, "but you're ever so handy, Pudge."

After persuading kindly old Mr. Scrubbs at the bank to sell them the house for $15,000 and the promise of their first-born child, Pudge armed himself with $27.58 worth of hammers, nails, and a big ball of twine. Within a fortnight, Pudge hung the finishing touch, an exact reproduction of the chandelier in Mount Vernon, which he had fashioned out of two-hundred lids of discarded Maxwell House coffee cans.

Another formidable item in their budget is food, which runs to a whopping $105 a month. "Babsie can make hamburger taste like filet mignon," the article quotes Pudge as saying. Of course, Babsie grows and cans her own vegetables. They evidently don't have problems with weevils and gophers; if they do, resourceful Babsie presumably cans them, too. They're probably what Pudge mistakes for filet mignon.

Naturally Babsie sews, and when she isn't putting up gophers, she's fashioning Dior copies out of sugar sacks and old bedsheets.

"Of course they manage on $412.76," I announced after reading the article. "Their children's teeth came in straight."

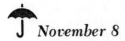 *November 8*

Undoubtedly one of the most difficult adjustments in a marriage is learning how to breathe.

Of course, breathing during the day is relatively simple, even for newlyweds. The problem arises only at night when one attempts to breathe in a double bed.

Unison Breathing: Initially you attempt to breathe in unison. You soon discover that, although otherwise you are perfectly well-suited to each other, you breathe at wildly divergent rates. Some find that to retain a semblance of unison they must pant like an exhausted Great Dane; others, married to deep breathers, turn blue.

Tandem Breathing: Besides involving all the timing problems of union breathing, the carbon dioxide exchange occurring during face-to-face tandem breathing (otherwise known as inhaling each other's exhale) is not beneficial unless one of you is a plant.

Regular Breathing: Eventually, about 2:00 A.M., you resolve to revert to regular breathing. Unfortunately, although you have been regular-breathing successfully for over twenty years, you find that suddenly this automatic reflex has become a strangely foreign exercise. "In goes the good air," you murmur, "out goes the bad air." It invariably feels as if you're doing it all wrong.

By now your bed partner is blissfully asleep, completely unaware that you have lost a vital bodily function. He is not only asleep, but snoring. Isn't that cute? Just like a saw. "Ah-whoof, Ah-whoof." Such a regular rhythm. "Ah-whoof, Ah-whoof, Ah." The sudden absence of a corresponding "whoof" jolts you from semi-consciousness, and you leap to all fours, certain that he has experienced a cardiac arrest. Just as you begin to attempt mouth-to-mouth resuscitation, he "whoofs" into your nose.

It may help to console yourself with the fact that, given ten or twelve years, you may become accustomed to breathing in a double bed. While not necessarily true, it may help you get to sleep.

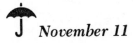 *November 11*

As I remember, it all started when I refused to let him eat

lunch with his hockey helmet on.

The situation deteriorated rapidly during a lecture en-titled "I'm Fully Aware that Creamed Chip Beef on Toast is Not Your Favorite Meal, But This Doesn't Happen to Be the Army, and Don't You Ever Call It That Again."

An hour later, wearing blue ski pajamas and his hockey helmet, he confronted us in the living room.

"You don't have to pretend any more," he announced gravely. "I know."

"He *knows!*" I gasped, icy fingers of panic clutching at my heart.

"Omigosh!" my husband replied, his face ashen. We sat in stunned silence for thirty seconds.

"Do you have any idea what he's talking about?" I finally asked.

"Not the slightest," my husband admitted.

"I'm adopted, amn't I?" our son said.

"What ever gave you that idea?"

"If I were your own little boy, you wouldn't pick on me all the time."

I was momentarily tempted to remind him that if he weren't our own little boy, we'd have given him back five years ago.

"Of course you're not adopted," my husband replied. "I'll show you your birth certificate to prove it."

"Besides," I reminded him, "being adopted doesn't mean that your parents don't love you. Being adopted means being chosen by two people who want that particular baby more than anything else in the world. They choose him out of all the other babies to take home with them and love."

"See," added his father, who had finally located our son's birth certificate in a folder containing the warranty on the blender. "You weren't adopted."

To our surprise, our son took one look at his birth certifi-cate and burst into tears.

"If I were your chosen child," he sobbed, "you wouldn't pick on me all the time."

J *November 12*

Last week our daughter announced that she would like to have a party.

"How about a Thanksgiving party," I suggested. "The girls could come as Indians or pilgrims."

"I want to have a mixed party," she replied.

"What do the girls come as at a mixed party?" my husband asked me.

"About half of them come as boys."

"Boys!?" he gasped.

"You know, snips and snails and puppy dogs' tails."

During the week before the party he took to wandering aimlessly around the house murmuring "Boys!?" in a stricken voice, as if we were about to be visited with an incurable disease.

For safety's sake, we held the party in the basement, where the only vulnerable antique is the furnace.

"For heaven's sake, can't you quiet those kids down?" my husband bellowed at 9:00 P.M. "What in the world is going *on* down there?

Not wanting to appear obtrusive, I quickly stripped three beds, gathered up the not-very-dirty sheets, and stomped down to the basement, whistling loudly. A hush descended on everyone, even Sam, who had been using chopsticks to drum out "Bridge Over Troubled Waters" on the water heater.

"Just going to wash out a few things," I explained. "Try to hold the noise down a bit," I added casually as I disappeared into the laundry room.

Fifteen minutes later my husband began frowning.

"For heaven's sake, now I can't hear a thing!"

"Neither can I," I mused. "I hope the washing machine isn't broken."

"What in the world is going *on* down there?"

"What could possibly be going on? They're only thirteen years old."

"I *know* they're only thirteen, but they've had all those sex education courses!"

Just then our daughter bounded upstairs.

"What a great party!" she exclaimed. "I'm so glad I invited boys. They're teaching us to burp at will!"

☂ November 19

A difficult problem in any family lies in how to handle breaches of discipline.

As one of the manifestations of sibling rivalry is the delight of seeing your fellow sib get the tar swatted out of him, most children take perverse pleasure in reporting any and every questionable activity in the vague hope that it might turn out to be a punishable offense.

The acts reported during a typical day are as follows:

"Jimmy said *that word* again!"

"Debbie blew bubbles in her milk!"

"Jimmy ate paste!"

"Debbie took *three* Kleenexes to blow her nose!"

"Jimmy left the seat up again!"

At which time, mother, who by now wishes she'd stayed single, delivers a lecture entitled "Nobody Likes a Snitch."

Things are blissfully quiet for two days until a blue flame shoots across the living room, Jimmy loses his eyebrows, and the entire house is plunged into darkness for three hours.

Whereupon another lecture is delivered, entitled "Although Nobody Likes a Snitch, If Jimmy Is Sticking Bobby Pins in the Electric Outlet, *Tell* Me!"

☂ November 21

I am sure that somewhere there are married couples who can enjoy successful husband-and-wife projects.

If It's Raining

Actually, I am not all that sure, but I prefer to start on a note of optimism, however unlikely and farfetched.

One of the major difficulties a husband and wife face is the question of pace. While one views a project as a sort of random activity which one can turn to during an odd hour or two every third Tuesday if "Three's Company" is a rerun, the other is frantically dedicated to seeing the entire project completed by 4:30 that very afternoon.

Consequently, observing that they have no sandpaper, the former is given to solemnly intoning nauseating homilies such as "Anything Worth Doing Is Worth Doing Well," before absently wandering out into the kitchen for a cup of Ovaltine and a jelly bun.

The other half, meanwhile, is grimly determined to scrape paint off the darned rocker, no matter what, and tackles the job with a nail file.

The more casually-inclined of the two will wander back periodically, while munching on his jelly bun, to deliver his considered opinion that the other is going about the project *all wrong*, running the obvious risk of being impaled on the pointy end of a nail file.

Of course, one is forever reading articles about a couple named Charlie and Mibbs who have a joint workshop in the basement where they hole up every night and have a splendid time tie-dyeing lamp shades.

If the truth were told, I'm certain that they loathe every minute of it, and as often as not spend the greater part of the evening smacking each other with sheets of wet batik.

 *November 22*

"I can stay by myself," my daughter declared. "And for one dollar an hour, I'll even take care of 'It,'" she added, gesturing toward her brother, who retaliated by smashing her kneecap with a croquet mallet.

"If I leave you alone, there will be no eye gouging, hair pulling, or hitting below the belt. You will retire to neutral corners, refrain from spitting out of the upstairs windows, and there will be peace in the valley when I return or I'll belt you!"

The first time I left them alone, I carefully wrote down the telephone numbers of the police, ambulance, fire department, doctor, dentist, veterinarian, the Suicide Prevention Center, and Alcoholics Anonymous.

"Now, I'll be at the Bennetts," I concluded. "Call me if there's an emergency."

When I arrived at the Bennetts' house ten minutes later, they informed me that the children had called three times, saying it was urgent. I raced to the telephone.

"Whatsthematter?" I shrieked.

"Can I have a Popsicle?" my son asked.

They called twelve times during the next four hours, imparting the vital information that we were all out of bread, that Archie Bunker said "damn" and that the bathroom light had burned out, and asking a variety of questions ranging from what is a cesarean section to what was for dinner tomorrow night.

"Look," I said to them the next day. "Call me for emergencies, not just to ask what Grandma's middle name is."

"What's an emergency?" my daughter asked.

"Blood, fire, explosion, rape, pillage—that sort of thing."

The next week I left them alone again. I had just arrived at the party when I received a phone call.

"Boy, what an explosion and fire!" my son began.

"What!?!"

"Yeah. I bet that Edith and Archie Bunker don't even have insurance!"

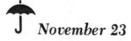 *November 23*

I remember Fred Allen. I remember Studebakers. I remember white washbowls with two faucets and two taps marked "H" and "C," when washing up involved whisking your hands rapidly between the two and having them alternately parboiled and frozen.

Fred Allen is dead. Studebakers are out of production. And last night I found myself alone in a strange bathroom, staring blankly at a washbowl with no faucets or taps, only a single chrome wheel.

I considered seeking assistance from my hostess who, presumably, had mastered the art of procuring water from a wheel. But, noticing the distinctive aroma of three dozen burned crab puffs, accompanied by the anguished wail "What do you mean, we're *out* of *ice*?!" I decided that my hostess had problems enough.

By resting my head in the washbowl and peering up, I discovered that there was an opening under the wheel for the water to flow through. A bit more assured, I stood up and pressed the center of the wheel gingerly with my index finger. Nothing.

Next I grasped the wheel firmly and pushed. Still nothing. Finally I attempted to turn it. In desperation I pulled the wheel, whereupon a torrent of scalding water dashed into the bowl and began ricocheting onto the bathroom mirror, the front of my dress, a box of facial tissues, and a paint-by-number picture of the Lord's Supper.

My hostess, possibly reasoning that we were her husband's friends and a shifty lot at best, had hidden all her bath towels, providing instead three tissue paper hand towels—featuring pictures of purple mice peering out of martini glasses—which disintegrated immediately upon contact with water.

Fortunately I have resourcefulness. I also have ingenuity. I have everything, in fact, but a cotton half-slip to replace the wet one I left in their tub after using it to wipe up the bathroom.

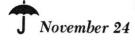 *November 24*

Winter driving is tricky.
The following are some typical winter driving problems

and their logical solutions.

Problem: You have gone to the veterinarian to get the dog's worm medicine. When you return to the car, you find that the plow has been past and there is nine inches of snow behind each rear tire. You attempt to back out, but your wheels spin helplessly.

Solution: You must put something under the back wheels to add necessary traction. An ingenious solution is to use your coat. An even more ingenious solution is to use someone else's coat.

Problem: You are twenty miles from home in a raging snowstorm, returning from the hairdresser who Mildred claimed was a magician, wearing a red woolen ski hat pulled down as far as it will go. The engine begins to go "Plick-plick-plick."

Solution: Pull into a gas station and knowledgeably explain to the attendant that you in all probability have an icy piston. After inspecting the car, he will reply that you have a Popsicle stick caught in the fan belt. He will snicker. Do not tip him.

November 25

I find that as we are approaching Thanksgiving, I have many things for which to be thankful. Having to cook a twenty-pound turkey is not among them.

Though normally they rank fairly high on my list of blessings, my children are no help at Thanksgiving, as they tend to hang about the kitchen all morning demanding freshly-squeezed orange juice and blueberry waffles when all I am able to concentrate on is wresting a bag of frozen giblets from a turkey that I had believed was completely thawed.

The distressing fact of the matter is that you simply cannot

158   *If It's Raining*

roast a turkey which still contains a cellophane bag full of liver. Even if you fully intend to throw the cellophane bag and everything in it down the garbage disposal, it still must come out of the turkey if you're to have any room for the stuffing.

The stuffing, of course, is another problem.

There is something infinitely pathetic about watching someone whose eyes are glued shut with last night's mascara standing over a hot cutting board at 8:30 A.M., chopping onions. You would think that at such moments any child with a shred of human decency would resist the temptation to bound around the kitchen, demanding to dissect the turkey's heart.

Once the children are breakfasting on hastily poured bowls of Rice Krispies, I reluctantly force down a sample of dressing, trying, usually unsuccessfully, to avoid the oysters.

"Is the stuffing good?" they demand.

"Super," I shudder, washing it down with a glass of prune juice.

"Gee, I wish we were having hamburgers instead."

☂ *December 1*

For two children who can never seem to recall where they've left their shoes, my offspring have remarkable memories for personal injustices.

It isn't as if I haven't tried to be fair. Anyone who spends twenty minutes measuring the one cherry in a bowl of fruit cocktail with a micrometer, so that she can cut it into two exactly equal halves, can hardly be accused of playing favorites.

Over the years I have come to the sad realization that being a mother is just like being a Supreme Court justice, only the pay is worse.

It is all I can do to decide what to fix for dinner, without having to act as the final authority on who gets to open the can that it's in.

"We've had the electric can opener for four days, and I've never *once* gotten to use it," my daughter complained.

"So what?" countered her brother. "Mom let *you* dissect the turkey heart last week."

"When we were little, you were always the one who got to ride in the grocery cart."

"Yeah, but she let *you* take the dog's baby teeth to school for Show-and-Tell."

"Maybe so, but Mom always gave *you* the rubber bands from the morning paper."

"That's not because Mom loves me best. That's because whenever she gave you one, you ate it."

🌂 *December 2*

I don't know the practice in your school district, but where we live, approximately twenty days out of every year are given over to Professional Development Days.

As the teaching staff obviously cannot develop professionally while simultaneously grappling with square roots, iambic pentameter, and the principal exports of Uruguay, everyone under eighteen is afforded a holiday.

While children eventually adapt to prolonged lack of regimentation during their summer vacation, they are ill-equipped to deal with a sudden one-day break in routine.

As a public service, I would like to offer my children's list of "What to Do on Professional Development Day."

1. Get up at 8:00 A.M. and watch your mother do her Bend-and-Stretch. Ask her how she got those wiggly red lines in the backs of her knees.
2. Wash your hair.
3. Start a batch of cardamom cookies.
4. Have Mom drive you to the store to buy cardamom.
5. Vacuum your guinea pig.
6. Watch "As the World Turns" and make retching noises.
7. Wash your hair again.
8. Count the number of raisins in a box of Raisin Bran.
9. Hold a Kiss Rock Festival.
10. Make an Evil Potion of milk of magnesia, Hawaiian Punch, and Clearasil.
11. Try to get your brother to drink it.
12. Paint your shoes.

J *December 3*

    One of the distressing aspects of an otherwise festive season is the inevitable necessity of choosing a Christmas card.

    Somehow I find that I must choose between the following types:

    Nostalgia Cards: A typical nostalgia card features a two-hundred-year-old stone house with a wisp of smoke rising from the chimney. Nostalgia cards are based on the dubious premise that there was something essentially festive, even ennobling, about plucking a bullet-ridden goose while snowbound in an isolated cottage.

    Symbolic Chic Cards: A typical symbolic chic card is white cardboard emblazoned with a stark sprig of holly embossed in fourteen-carat gold. The sentiment inside is a Spartan "Seasons Greetings" above a printed name, evoking the same good cheer as an announcement of a corporate merger.

    Cutesy Cards: Cutesy cards invariably feature pictures of white mice wearing Santa Claus suits climbing out of empty martini glasses, reindeer with kegs of brandy around their necks, or three rabbits peering into a manger at the Christ Child, who bears a startling resemblance to a Chatty Cathy doll.

    Folksy Cards: Folksy cards are preprinted with color photographs of the senders taken in July while standing in front of their twenty-foot sloop, 1978 Lincoln Continental, or a quaint little shop on the outskirts of Istanbul. These cards are especially depressing when received by a person who spent July driving a ten-year-old Dodge back and forth to a son's trombone lesson.

    Old Masters Cards: An old masters card features a sloe-eyed Virgin Mary holding a chubby Jesus whose eyes have been printed off-center. The card, printed in old English script, reads "May the Peace of Jefuf live in your heartf."

If It's Raining

J *December 9*

I took my children to Chicago to visit my mother and all my relatives, an event, I fear, rather like casting swine before pearls.

"You can do your own packing," I said to my daughter. "But I don't want to see any green nail polish, bleached jeans, or sweatshirts that say 'I Like Being a Sex Object.' Don't you have anything with puffed sleeves and smocking?"

"I thought you wanted us to be ourselves," she complained.

"Of course not! Are you out of your mind?" I exclaimed. "And you," I said, turning to my son. "In Chicago you wear pajamas to bed, not your underwear. Here, take these," I added, handing him seven monogrammed handkerchiefs.

"What are these?" he asked.

"They're for blowing your nose."

"Cloth Kleenex!" he exclaimed. "What will they think of next?"

Early on departure day, we frantically distributed house keys, African Violets, and gerbils to semiwilling neighbors, arriving at the airport an hour early for our flight. My son decided to while-away the time by sitting between a pair of skis and a green two-suiter. I wouldn't have minded, but they happened to be on a luggage conveyor belt at the time. I plucked him off smartly as he went past.

"Why don't you go watch TV?" I suggested, a note of desperation creeping into my voice.

"What's on?"

"An award-winning drama called 'Arrival and Departure Times.' You'll love it," I assured them.

"Now for heaven's sake," I cautioned them as we finally boarded the plane, "watch your language at Grandma's house!"

"You mean we can't say %!&N or ••$&?"

"*Especially* not ••$&," I exclaimed. "By the way, what's

that bulge in your pocket?"

"A gerbil," he admitted.

"Oh °°$&" I sighed.

"I certainly hope they've corrected the basic structural fault that they discovered in these planes last month," my daughter remarked in the tone of voice one normally reserves for calling hogs, as we boarded the plane.

A blanket of silence fell over the entire economy class, followed by a rustle, as morning newspapers (whose owners realized might be final editions) slipped from nerveless fingers. Seventeen people ordered double martinis on the spot. Six others demanded that the stewardess baptize them.

"What do you know about basic structural faults?" I whispered to my daughter.

"Nothing," she grinned. "But I sure got them going, didn't I?"

The flight passed uneventfully, except for us each getting five lunches, thanks to an inexplicable lack of appetite among the other passengers.

Now, seeing them every day, a parent tends to forget how very much children can change during one year. We arrived at O'Hare Airport to find my mother anxiously peering through the arrival gate.

"Where are my babies?" she demanded, after giving me a decidedly perfunctory kiss on the cheek.

"Do you see those two enormous girls following me?" I asked.

"Yes."

"Well, the girl with the shorter hair is your grandson."

"Hi, Grandma," he said. "I'm hungry."

"You'll have to excuse him," I explained. "We had rather an exciting flight, and he hasn't eaten for two hours."

Being exposed to a large, urban metropolis like Chicago is an exhilarating experience for a child. Unfortunately, in a ninth-floor, one-bedroom apartment, two exhilarated children are approximately as welcome as a fungus infection. It

If It's Raining

becomes a question of keeping them occupied. My children solved the problem of potential boredom by jamming pins in the emergency-stop button on the elevator, throwing pennies down the incinerator, and telling each other dirty jokes over the intercom.

After this paled, they began rummaging through Mother's refrigerator.

"What's to eat?" my son asked.

"You can't eat now!" my mother exclaimed. "We're going out to dinner in a restaurant in an hour. If you eat now, you'll spoil your dinner."

"Mother!" I protested. "That's the whole idea!"

During the next four days, the highpoints for the children were the hot-fudge sundaes we had after touring the Natural History Museum, the foot-long hotdogs we ate before going to the Science Museum, and the barbecued beefburgers we smuggled past the guard and ate while touring the aquarium.

"I want this trip to be something you'll never forget," my mother said to the children. "Chicago is just full of fascinating educational attractions. What else would you like to see?"

"The Playboy Club," suggested my son.

"How about the scene of the St. Valentine's Day Massacre?" my daughter offered.

"Look, if we visit one more tourist attraction, I'll burst," I complained. "Besides, we leave tomorrow. I have to pack."

"I sure hate to see you go," my mother said.

"Don't think of it as losing your grandchildren. Think of it as getting your refrigerator back."

 *December 12*

A great deal has been written about the loss of the true meaning of Christmas. As an aid to those of you who are disgusted by crass commercialism, I offer the following step-by-step instructions on "How to Have an Old-Fashioned Christmas."

1. December 10—Buy a live goose. Call him Sylvester. Tie him to the water heater in the basement. Encourage the children to play with him and teach him tricks.

2. December 15—Choose a day when it's thirty degrees below zero to go out and cut your own Christmas tree. Don't cut the first tree you see. Tromp through the whole forest looking for a better one. *Then* come back and cut the first tree you saw.

3. December 16—String popcorn and cranberries to decorate the tree, using heavy thread and a very sharp needle. Try to bleed only on the cranberries, where it won't show.

4. December 17—Invite both of your entire families to spend the holidays with you. Even Uncle Frank, whom no one has mentioned since he voted for Roosevelt.

5. December 18—Give the milkman and the paperboy shiny dimes for Christmas. The look of wonder in their eyes will reflect their sincere intention of giving you truly unbelievable service during the coming year.

6. December 19—Organize a skating party on the river. Be careful not to trip over the raw sewage.

7. December 23—Kill Sylvester. Pluck him and make a pillow.

8. December 24—Turn off the furnace before you go to bed, ensuring that Christmas morning will find everyone blue with cold and unable to use the bathroom because the pipes are frozen solid.

9. December 25—Arise promptly at 5:00 A.M. Stuff the goose. Cook it in an iron stove with faulty dampers. Later, give each of the children a pair of too-large handknit mittens and an orange.

 *December 16*

Call me a slave to tradition, but each year I insist upon having a real Christmas tree. The kind that gets sap all over your hands and drops long needles that clog up the vacuum cleaner.

To me there is nothing very festive about assembling a boxed Christmas tree. I know that they are fireproof, more perfect that nature, and a savings in the long run, but they don't *smell* like Christmas trees. It's the sap that smells. Of course, sap gets all over your hands and we're back where we started.

My family humors me in this harmless idiosyncrasy as one might a senile uncle who saves toothpaste caps. I'm not really bothering anyone, and my little fetish does provide lots of laughs:

"Your Christmas tree is all sticky."

"That's sap."

"What's 'sap'?"

"Ask my mother."

Humoring my hang-up doesn't include assisting with the purchase, however. After all, no one helps senile uncles look for toothpaste caps. As soon as little forests start sprouting around the shopping center, I whip on my longjohns for another lonely quest. My system involves starting with the Boy Scouts ten miles away and working back toward home, past the Women of the Moose and the Baptist Church.

Last year the routing was similar, but the temperature was zero when I set out. Six lots and two hours later, the mercury had tumbled to ten below, and the only might-do-in-a-pinch trees were three dollars a foot. My eyelashes were frozen together by then, and I'd lost all feeling in my left foot. Ending up at my last hope, the Baptist Church, I had to decide finally whether to get a twelve dollar Douglas fir that was tall enough but shaped like a mushroom, or a gorgeous seven-foot Scotch Pine that was twenty dollars. Impetuously, I bought the Scotch Pine, wondering vaguely how I'd serve the Christmas meatloaf.

By the time I got home, my family had evidently given up hope of seeing me alive again and were getting ready to go out to dinner.

"Well, I got one."

"Another sticky one?"

"That's sap."

"What's 'sap'?"

Ask your mother, she's one.

☂ December 26

While a vast amount of literary effort and advertising promotion has been expended in extolling the merriment of Christmas Eve and Christmas morning, very little, if anything, has ever been written about Christmas afternoon.

But, yes, Virginia, there is a Christmas afternoon. It exists as surely as does a second day of school, a fifty-first wedding anniversary, and the day after two glorious weeks in Acapulco.

☂ December 27

Friday, December 14

My Dearest True Love:

Along with the orthodontist's bill for $75.50 and three Christmas cards from total strangers, I received your pear tree today. You shouldn't have. I mean, every time I look at it (which of necessity is fairly often, as it takes up half the living room), I think of you. Oh, yes, I almost forgot to mention the enchanting little Cornish hen perched on one branch. Absolutely charming. A little stringy, perhaps, but a welcome change from hamburger.

Saturday, December 15

My Dear True Love:

Gosh! Another pear tree. Another stringy Cornish hen,

If It's Raining

too. Have I ever mentioned how badly I need a new steam iron? Until our son builds a coop for the pigeons, I'm keeping them in the coat closet.

Sunday, December 16
Dear True Love:
We couldn't coax today's Cornish hen out of the tree; he justs sits there on the top branch and throws pears at us. Thank heavens the coop is finished; you should see what those pigeons did to my hat. By the way, those three chickens you sent are terribly high-strung. They leaped out of the box, shrieked "Mon Dieu!" and ran under the sofa.

Tuesday, December 18
Dear T.L.:
I'm sorry that I didn't write yesterday, but since our son has lost interest in pigeons, I had to clean the coop myself. I was delighted with the five rings. I didn't know that there was such a thing as two-carat gold.

Wednesday, December 19
Hi:
We chopped today's tree into kindling, which so frightened the Cornish hen that he flew through the picture window. The geese have made themselves quite at home, so much so that they follow us around, nipping at our heels like puppies— big puppies! Big untrained puppies! I finally understand what is meant by the phrase "loose as a goose."

Thursday, December 20
My Dear True Love:
Today the post office delivered seven swans. They have been temporarily billeted in the bathtub, where they are unsuccessfully attempting to mate with the rubber duck.

Friday, December 21
Dear T.L.:
I was ecstatic today to be greeted by eight maids. Un-

fortunately they refused to deal with the mess that the birds have created. They insist on milking. In view of the fact that good help is so hard to come by, could you see your way clear to sending us a cow?

Saturday, December 22
My Dear Sir:
I was puzzled and dismayed today to receive nine members of British nobility, when what I really needed was a cow. When they aren't busy bounding over the furniture, they are engaging in an unseemly amount of slap and tickle with the maids, who are not remotely interested in milking anymore.

Monday, December 24
Sir:
Regarding your gifts of the past two days, the last thing I need is thirty-one additional houseguests. Especially since the bathtub is full of swans. Besides, I am not overly fond of bagpipes, believing in fact that the only good bagpipe is a dead bagpipe. It is impossible to concentrate on the morning paper with eleven pipers marching around the breakfast table, followed by twenty girls frugging to "Loch Lomond."

Tuesday, December 25
Now Hear This!
With the arrival today of twelve bongo players, there are now 140 people drumming, piping, dancing, leaping and not milking. Not to mention 184 birds (less the two we ate and the one that flew through the picture window), doing birdlike things such as picking lice out of their tails.
I am returning all forty golden rings. The engagement is *off*! Do you hear me? *Off*!